Franz von Suppé

Fatinitza

With Music and Illustrations by the Gravuretype Co.

Franz von Suppé

Fatinitza
With Music and Illustrations by the Gravuretype Co.

ISBN/EAN: 9783337088026

Printed in Europe, USA, Canada, Australia, Japan

Cover: Foto ©Thomas Meinert / pixelio.de

More available books at **www.hansebooks.com**

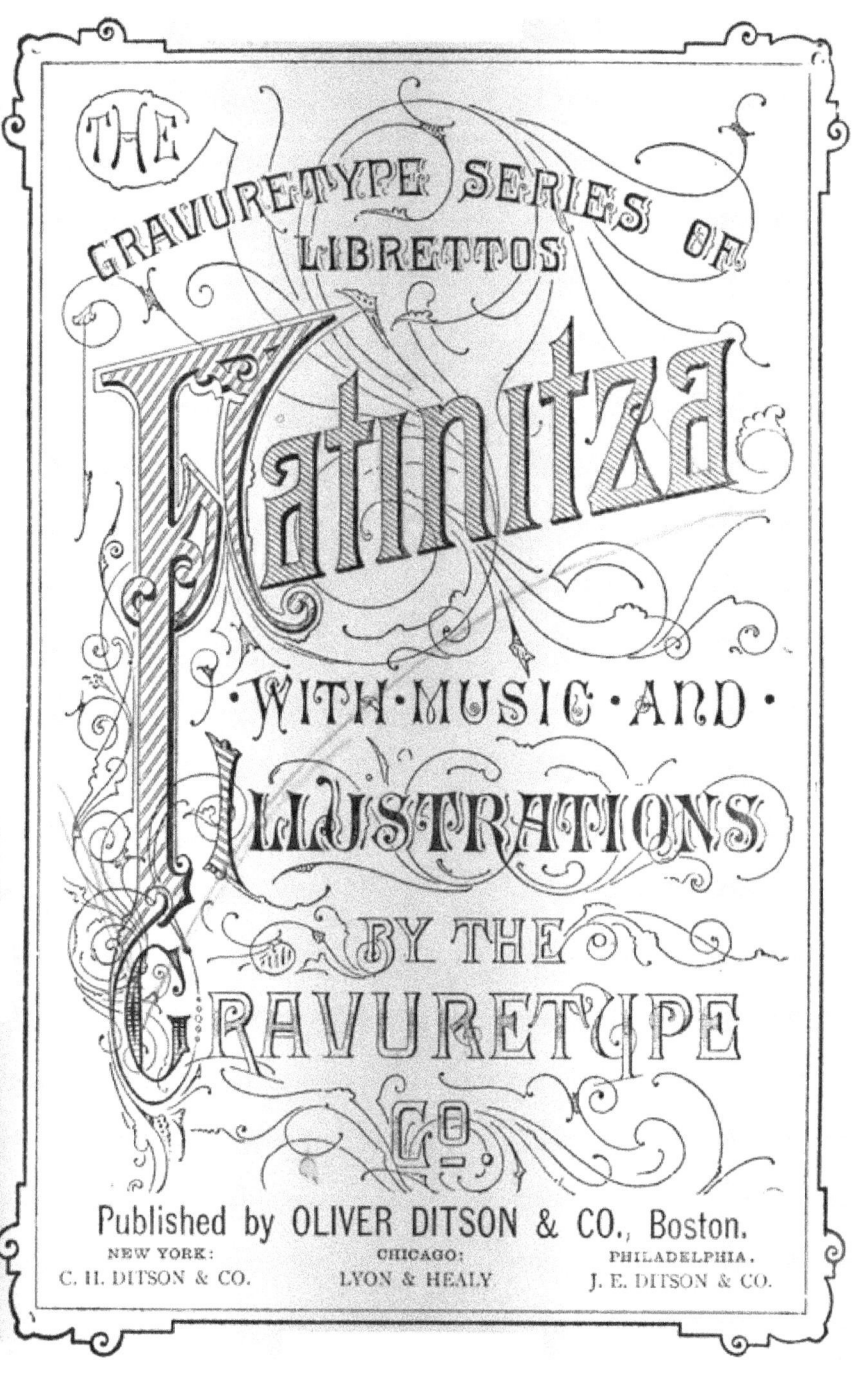

ARGUMENT.

A HANDSOME and very youthful lieutenant of a Circassian regiment in the Russian army, named Vladimir Samoiloff, while masquerading in girl's dress under the name of Fatinitza, is met by a rough old general, Count Timofey Kantchukoff, who falls violently in love with him. Vladimir extricates himself from this dilemma, and afterwards, in Odessa, meets the general's niece, the Princess Lydia Imanovna, whom he knows only as Lydia; and the two form a romantic attachment. Hearing of this, the old general has the young officer transferred to the outposts of the Russian army on the Danube.

The piece opens with a scene in camp before Rustchuk. After some characteristic military scenes, during which Vladimir tells the story of his love for Lydia, an American newspaper special correspondent, Julian Hardy, the good genius of about everybody in the piece, is brought on by the Cossacks as a spy, but is recognized by Vladimir as an old friend. To relieve the ennui of camp-life, he proposes that they have some private theatricals,—a suggestion which is hailed with delight. Vladimir agrees to play the "leading lady;" and, while all the company has retired to dress for the rehearsal, Gen. Kantchukoff arrives unexpectedly. He pounces upon Julian, who escapes by showing his passports, and quite gets the better of the old general by his professional impudence. Vladimir then comes on in peasant-girl's attire, and is recognized by the general as his first and only love, Fatinitza. Then come the cadets, soldiers, and officers, disguised in all sorts of absurd costumes, to the great astonishment and intense rage of the general, who is, however, conciliated by the pretended Fatinitza, who coaxes him to let the offenders go. Glad to be left alone with his love, the general orders them off to drill; but his love-making is interrupted by the announcement of the arrival of his niece, the Princess Lydia, whose noble rank is thus first revealed to Vladimir, who fears recognition in his disguise. Complications are again smoothed over by the correspondent, who explains the resemblance by telling the princess that Fatinitza is her lover Vladimir's sister. The general commends Fatinitza to the princess, and goes off to inspect the troops. A band of Bashi-Bazouks then steal upon the scene, surprise the Russian works, and capture the princess, Vladimir, and Julian; leaving the latter behind, however, to arrange for ransom for their captives. Just as they are going, the Russian troops return, but are prevented from firing upon the retreating Turks by the general, for fear that they "might hit Fatinitza!"

The second act shows us the harem of the reform Turk, Izzet Pasha, the governor of the Turkish fortress; and there are some comical scenes with his family of four wives. Vladimir, still in woman's guise, and Lydia are brought in as captives; and the Pasha announces to his four "better-halves" that he is about to add Lydia to their number, much to their vexation. Then comes Julian, with the Russian Sergeant Steipann, to arrange for the release of the captives. The Pasha is willing to give up Fatinitza, but refuses to part with Lydia. Steipann is despatched to carry the Pasha's terms to the general, with a secret message from Julian telling how he can surprise the Turks with his army; Julian having obtained the knowledge from Vladimir, who, in a previous scene, has declared his identity to Lydia, and also to the four wives, whom he persuades to abet their escape. Julian is left as the guest of the Pasha, and the two have a very jolly time together. A "Karagois," or Turkish shadow-pantomime, is gotten up for the entertainment of the strangers; but it is given an unlooked-for conclusion by the arrival of the Russians, who come to rescue their friends.

The third act takes place in the general's summer-palace near Odessa. The princess has been promised by the general to a maimed and crippled old friend of his; but Julian arrives with Vladimir, and, through the ingenuity of the former, matters are smoothed over: and the general, who finds in the Fatinitza whose coming he has been impatiently expecting nothing but a veiled negress bearing that name, is made to believe that the real Fatinitza has died of grief at her separation from him, and so he consents to the union of her brother Vladimir, whom she commits to his care in a parting letter, with his niece.

CHARACTERS OF THE OPERA.

COUNT TIMOFEY GAVRILOVITCH KANTCHUKOFF, *Russian General.*
PRINCESS LYDIA IMANOVNA, *his Niece.*
IZZET PASHA, *Governor of the Turkish Fortress at Rustchuk.*
CAPTAIN VASIL STARAVIEFF.
LIEUTENANT OSIPP SAFONOFF.
IVAN,
NIKIPHAR,
FEDOR,
DIMITRI, } *Cadets.*
WASILI,
MICHALOFF,
CASIMIR,
GREGOR,
STEIPANN, *Sergeant.*
VLADIMIR SAMOILOFF, *Lieutenant of a Circassian Cavalry Regiment.*
JULIAN HARDY, *Special War Correspondent of the "New-York Herald."*
HASSAN BEY, *Leader of a Squad of Bashi-Bazouks.*
NURSIDAH,
ZULEIKA,
DIONA, } *Izzet Pasha's Wives.*
BESIKA,
MUSTAPHA, *Guardian of the Harem.*
VUIKA, *a Bulgarian.*
HANNA, *his Wife.*
A COSSACK.
A MILITARY COOK.

THE ABDUCTION OF FATINITZA BY THE TURKS.
(PATENT APPLIED FOR.)

FATINITZA.

ACT FIRST.

AT THE OUTPOSTS.

In the Russian camp on the Lower Danube. Winter

INTRODUCTION.

GUARD (*on the right*).
Who goes there? Attention, all!
GUARD (*in left wing*).
Who goes there? Attention, all!

STEIPANN.
Get up! Ho, there! ye lazy knaves.
Already day is here—hurry up!
The drum to wake is beating—
To wake, the trumpet calls!
Up, ye cowards! where's your hearing?
Form in steady martial bearing.
   Up be going—
   Late 'tis growing;
   How much more noise
   Must I devise
   To make you rise?

When in robes of white earth lies before me,
Bright with frost and snow, delight comes o'er me!
Then, in icy fetters though she's bound,
Russia stands, a queen, with splendor crowned.
   Shivering with the cold—Brrrrrr—
   When the whist'ling winds I hear,
   Blow as if to split the ear—
Ten thousand bombs! ah, what delight!
No Russian is he, who feels it not aright.
Those cadets—deuce take them! sleeping—
From their beds they're not yet creeping;
Heard they not the call that sounded?

(*Hit by a snowball.*)

But what is this? I am confounded.

(*Cadets steal on to the stage, and bombard* STE-
IPANN *with snowballs.*)

STEIPANN.
To great a liberty it is
To allow such a row—
No, 'twould to duty be remiss.
There, enough! Come, be quiet!
No; I, forsooth, will not submit.
Leave me alone; I yield me now—
One against you all.
I yield and to your valor bow.
However nice,
It seems to me this may suffice.
Hold up! hold up!
It seems to me that this must stop—
This now must stop, I say;
Or else, in truth, there'll something be to pay.
If one alone in hand should be,
He will have work to do with me.

CADETS.
Ha, ha, ha! Be on your guard; come on!
Now, bravely—piff, paff!—he's yielding!
Piff, paff!—He can resist us not much more.
Hurrah! Come onward—piff, paff!
Still on he goes in speedy flight;
For pity asks the coward wight!
Ha, ha, ha, ha! he yields—all right!
Ha, ha, ha, ha! what valor bright!
   We've hurried him,
   And worried him Hurrah!
When in robes of white, &c., &c.

(STEIPANN *runs off.*)

ALL CADETS.
Ha, ha, ha! Hurrah!

OSIPP.
Hey, there, you rogues!

IVAN.
The lieutenant! Good morning, lieutenant.

ALL.
Good morning!

OSIPP.
Good morning! You are no longer in the academy youngsters. Here, in the great military school before the enemy, you must leave off your boyish pranks.

IVAN.
Beg pardon, lieutenant. We were only having a little fun.
OSIPP (*pleasantly*).
Well, I can't blame you. There is really little fun to be had here in the outposts before Rustschuk, looking out for these devilish Turks.
IVAN.
Nothing to eat at that!
FEODOR.
Nothing to drink!
NIKIPHAR.
No balls!
WASILI.
No theatres!
DIMITRI (*the youngest of all*).
No women!
OSIPP.
Women! Why, Dimitri! You must be thinking of your nurse, you little fragment of a soldier!
(*All laugh.*)
DIMITRI.
Oho! The grand Duke is here on the Danube with forty-five thousand men. If I were not a whole man, then you would say forty-four thousand nine hundred and ninety-nine and a half men; *ergo* I am a whole man. (*All laugh.*)
OSIPP.
So, you whole man, reach us your brandy-flask; mine is empty.
DIMITRI.
Mine too! (*Music.*)
IVAN.
Just in time! Here comes a sutler!
(*Joyful commotion.*)
ALL.
A sutler! Bravo! (*The soldiers in the background utter cries of joy, and rush to meet* VUIKA *who enters* R.)
(*Entrance of sutlers.* VUIKA *driving a dog-sled loaded with casks of liquor, baskets and other sutler's wares. He repeats his call on entering. His wife shoves the sled from behind. Both have characteristic make-ups, gypsy-like costumes, feet wrapped in strips of cloth; ragged, and very servile in manner.*)
VUIKA.
Whiskey here—who wants to buy?
Health and strength it will supply.
(*Soldiers surround the sled tumultuously; hold out their canteens. The woman serves them. Music stops.*)
OSIPP.
Well, now, what are the Turks doing over there?
VUIKA.
Me not know! Me not know, Gospod (*cunningly*). But, yes! Yesterday did the Turks try to come over the frozen Danube, and—hahaha! ice break!
OSIPP.
So, if the ice had not been weak, we should have had a surprise.
VUIKA (*shrugs shoulders.*)
Surprise, Gospod, ah! Moslem no courage, and only four hundred man.
DIMITRI (*murmurs*).
So! just double the strength of our pickets!
VUIKA (*aside*). Just what I wanted to know.
CAPT. VASIL.
Dimitri Fedorowich!

THE OTHERS.
The captain! (*Salute in unison.*) Good morning, captain.
VASIL.
Good morning! (*To* DIMITRI.) Three days' barrack arrest for talking too much.
DIMITRI.
Captain!
VASIL.
Not a word more! Right about—march! And this scoundrel of a gypsy may go home to the devil!
VUIKA.
O Gospod! mercy—
VASIL.
Away with him! (*To the soldiers.*) Have you paid the woman?
ALL.
Yes, captain.
VASIL.
So then—*basta!*
OSIPP.
Twenty degrees below zero last night!
VASIL (*gaping*). It is devilish slow out here!
OSIPP. That is true!
STEIPANN (*Comes forward*).
Oh, I smell wutky!
IVAN (*offers his flask*).
Here, old Cartridge Case, have a drink.
THE OTHERS (*offering their canteens.*)
Drink! drink!
STEIPANN.
Slowly! slowly! Each man in his turn; order must be maintained. (*Drinks from each canteen.*)
VASIL (*in the meanwhile at cards*). Ivan!
IVAN (*salutes*). Captain!
VASIL.
How about breakfast? Who is the officer of the day?
IVAN (*in undertone*). Officer of the day?
FEDOR (*in undertone*). Lieut. Vladimir.
IVAN (*aloud*). Lieut. Vladimir.
VASIL (*continuing his game*).
Where in the devil is he?
FEDOR (*undertone to* IVAN). In bed!
IVAN.
In bed? We'll soon wake him! Our morning serenade at the academy!
CHORUS OF CADETS.
Still snoring, still asleep he's lying—
Tschin ta, ta, ra, ta!
Wake up! tis late—the hours are flying!
Tschin ta, ta, ra, ta!
Ope wide your eyes to day's bright beams,
And stop your snoring, and your dreams.
(VLADIMIR *enters from barracks, and shakes hands with his comrades.*)
DREAM SONG.
VLADIMIR.
Why, ah why did you thus wake me?
And from me rend such a sweet enchanting dream!
CADETS.
That is fine—fine, indeed!
VLADIMIR.
From my heart 'twill ne'er depart,
For it was a dream of love!
Yes, a dream that fancy wove—
CADETS.
Of a wife fair and mild?
Go on, go on, in tender style—
Describe your charming dream meanwhile.

STILL SNORING, &c.

FATINITZA.

VLADIMIR.

Charms, that visions thus unfold,
I may never more behold!
Her to the air around me,
My lip dares not yet name;
But she whose charms have bound me,
To me in visions came.
Sang she there with voice enchanting,
That caused my heart to move,
And throb with burning love,
Beneath her glances haunting.
She filled a cup with sparkling wine,
And gave me with a look divine;
With ardent passion burning,
My lip approached it yearning.
    Alas! O fortune capricious!
    That moment delicious
    Was lost with the dream!
O hapless fate! O hapless fate!
It vanished and fled with the dream!

CADETS.

What pity! It fled with the dream!

VLADIMIR.

O vision! the face so beaming,
Where pride and softness met,
A smile did send me; seeming
Love's message, "Ne'er forget!"
I felt the trembling pressure
Of her soft hand in mine—
Her breathing soft and fine,
I heard in fitful measure.
Our lips, one sole desire alights,
Our hearts one single vow unites;
    The witchery of her glances
    A langor soft enhances.
Alas! O fortune capricious, etc.

CADETS.

What pity! It fled with the dream.

VASIL.

(*After finishing the game, comes forward with* OSIPP. VLADIMIR *salutes.* VASIL *salutes*) You nave been dreaming, Vladimir?

VLADIMIR.

Yes. (*A very deep sigh.*) Ah!!!

VASIL.

A regular alarm gun of a sigh. Are you in love? Hey? (VLADIMIR *gives a melancholy nod.*)

VASIL.

Who is the fair one?

VLADIMIR.

I must keep the name a secret, Vasil!

DIMITRI.

(*Thrusting his head out of the barrack door.*) His sweetheart's name is Lydia. I heard it in his sleep. (*Disappears. The others laugh.*)

VASIL.

So her name is Lydia—a stage name?

VLADIMIR (*decidedly*).

Oh, no! she belongs to the aristocracy. (*Relates.*) While in Odessa, I broke my ankle in consequence of being thrown from my horse. The lady in question was driving past at the time, and in spite of the remonstrance of her companion, who called her Lydia Imanovna, she took me into her carriage, and brought me to my lodgings, whither she sent daily to ask after me. I had scarcely recovered when I was ordered here. Wherefore? And I have never been able to learn who she was.

VASIL.

You were placed under my command with the special remark that an officer in the army, in high position, had requested you to be transferred because his ward had looked too deeply into your eyes!

VLADIMIR.

The deuce!

OSIPP.

Poor fellow! banished to the outposts on account of your handsome eyes!

VLADIMIR (*in vexation*).

And if there were only a skirmish here once in awhile—a surprise from the enemy—some kind of occupation, but this—(*A loud noise outside* t*. The pickets call out "To arms!" All hurry to grasp their weapons; the artillerists hasten to the guns; the infantry form in line. A long roll of drums introduces the following.*)

REPORTER'S SONG.

STEIPANN.

What's that noise?

COSSACKS.

A spy! A spy!

STEIPANN.

Who can he be?

COSSACKS.

We'll see! We'll see.

JULIAN.

Ah! wait, while I explain.

COSSACKS.

He thinks we shall believe!

JULIAN.

But all know who I am!

COSSACKS.

Thou art a cut-throat knave!

JULIAN.

You honor me too much, my friends!

COSSACKS.

Thou art a spy that Turkey sends!

Cadets, Soldiers, Cossacks, STEIPANN, *with tenors.*

Let us hang him!

JULIAN.

O thank you for such favors kind!

CHORUS.

We will hang thee!

JULIAN.

I am grateful, though the boon's declined!

CHORUS.

By the neck!

JULIAN.

Ah, what delight!

CHORUS.

You soon shall see!

VLADIMIR (*recognizing him*).

Julian here!

FATINITZA.

Vladimir!

JULIAN.

CHORUS.

Who in the deuce, now, can he be?

VLADIMIR (*introducing him*).

Julian Golz—a writer for the press,
By Russians much esteemed.

JULIAN.

Employers sent me hither
With the special mission trusted
Of observing and recording
All the deeds of war progressing;
And 'tis thus you find me here,
A war reporter, by your leave!

CHORUS.

A reporter? What is that?

JULIAN.

A reporter, I propose,
Is a man who all things knows.
Stay, while I explain.
With my note-book every where,
Always ready, prompt and free,—
Here to-day, to-morrow there,—
Naught can be unknown to me.
Day by day I gather facts;
Every item that attracts
And awakes the reader's mind
Seeking out, I always find,—
Now with vigor, oft with grace,
But for falsehood find no place:
In my diary you'll see
Breathing actuality.
What has scarcely yet occurred
I compose and give it word;
What the future still conceals
I set upright on its heels;
Things to come I write out, giving
Some one dead who still is living,
And, in my succeeding letter,
Bring him to, and all goes better.
Here to-day, to-morrow gone;
Night and day still moving on.
There's no club, no boudoir free,
That can close its door to me;
To the font with babes I go,
At the altar kneel with brides,
At the funerals with the dead;
All of good or ill I heed.
Is one knighted at the court,
Should some guilty wretch be hung,
Both are things that find a tongue
In my dutiful report.
Balls in season I attend,
In balloons on high ascend;
Should a theft committed be,
Ere 'tis known to police 'tis known to me.
To the scenes of conflagrations
With the engine-men I run;
At processions and cremations,
Fights or feasts, I see the fun.
Meetings, sermons and flirtations,
Gay parades, illuminations,
Races, dances, revolutions,
Thé-dansants or executions;
Thus to all in turn I go,

All I see and all I know,—
Prima donnas, praise their art;
Dancers, good advice impart;
Rising genius, give renown,
Soon to see it tumble down;
Notice profits and applauses;
Plead of concertists the causes;
Singers' trials, gains and losses,
These have part in my profession.
Writing articles, reviewing,
And inventing oft at need,
If of faith 'tis worthy, showing
One to wonder at and heed.
Easy to find those whose wits are straying;
But thus the journalist is never caught,
Merry and steady, witty and ready,
Frank, and always with good humor fraught.
One, in short,
Whose trade, forsooth,
Is to knead with falsehood, truth,—
Wit in universal dress
Means a reporter for the press,
Who mingles truth with falsehood's lies,—
One day affirms, the next denies:
This, full of jovial happiness,
Is a reporter for the press.

CADETS.

In faith, that's good!
Original!—Sesquipedal!
Pyramidal; in fact, a knowing youth.
And hence we'll know, we here confess,
What means "Reporter for the press."

VASIL.

I beg your pardon, sir, for the extreme zeal of our Cossacks; but you can easily see—

JULIAN.

I can easily see! Don't mention it, captain. I am charmed and delighted at their slight mistake.

VLADIMIR.

How is that?

JULIAN.

Why, my dear sir, it will make a glorious special for the press. (*Business with note-book.*) "Pursuit and capture of our special correspondent by Cossacks!" "Brave but futile resistance!" "Rough sons of the North!" "Tough little ponies of the Steppes!" "Long lances!" "Dragged away at a tearing gallop!" "Threatened with the knout!" (*Salutes* VASIL.) "Commander a cultivated officer!" "Cordial reception!" "Bountiful dinner!" &c., &c. By Jove, sir, I can't do this adventure short of a column and a half!

VLADIMIR.

You will have to leave out that "bountiful dinner," old fellow: we have hardly a thing to eat ourselves.

HARDY.
So much the letter! What is the use of being war correspondent? Just wait for "The Herald" six weeks hence, and you will just wonder at the quantities of dainties you have set before me!

MILITARY COOK.
The *shtshee* is ready.

HARDY (*to* VLADIMIR).
Beg pardon, lieutenant; but *what* the dence was it they said was ready?

VLADIMIR (*laughs*).
The *shtshee* — our "bountiful dinner"!

HARDY.
Ah! so the *shtshee* is ——?

VALDIMIR.
A mixed-up mess of cabbage, beets, parsnips, gunpowder, mutton, &c. Between you and me, a dish for the dogs; but we have nothing else.
[*In background a corporal portions out the rations. The soldiers eat it with spoons from tin dishes.*]

HARDY.
Ah, thanks for your timely explanation! But tell me, can you drink allash with this so-called "*shtshee*"?

VLADIMIR.
If we only had some at hand, to be sure —

HARDY.
Well, I'm your man then; for I happen to have two bottles in my bag. [*Goes to bag.*]

ALL OFFICERS (*joyfully*).
Allash! allash!
[HARDY *produces the bottles from his bag.*]

VLADIMIR.
Upon my word, friend, you are developing qualities which fill us all with the deepest respect.

VASIL.
What lucky star leads you to us?

HARDY.
This lucky star is called "journalistic enterprise." The editor wrote to me, "Are you observing the movements of the Turks?" Well, I have been observing the movements of the Turks through my field-glass!

VLADIMIR.
And what kind of movements did they make?

HARDY.
I saw standing on the banks of the beautiful blue Danube — which happens to be green wherever I have seen it — a Moslem who was doing so [*business of hopping from one foot to another, slapping the arms together, and breathing between the fingers like a man half frozen*].

VASIL.
So you can simply write to your paper, "The Turks are freezing!"

HARDY.
Captain, how little you comprehend the descriptive powers of a "Herald" correspondent! I write, heavily underscored, "Postscript! — In consequence of personal observations, I am enabled to inform you that the Turkish army is in motion [*hops as before*], and is taking comprehensive measures [*slaps his arms together*] to defy the rigors of a winter campaign!"

VASIL.
And in this way history is made. Long live "The Herald" correspondent!

ALL.
Hurrah!
DIMITRI (*looks out from barracks*).
Ahem!

ALL.
What's the matter?

DIMITRI.
I haven't had a drop.

VASIL.
Well, come out, you rogue! we will forgive you. [*Introduces* DIMITRI *to* HARDY.] Dimitri Fedorowitch, the most indiscreet gosling in camp.

HARDY.
Young man, indiscretion is a virtue, which I appreciate highly. Let us be friends [*shaking hands*]. And now, gentlemen, let merriment be the order of the day. How do you manage to divert the monotony of camp routine?

VLADIMIR.
We eat, we drink; we drink, and we sleep. — when the Turks will let us.

HARDY.
Well — and the ladies?

VASIL.
With the exception of a few ancient gypsies, we have not seen a woman of any sort for three months.

HARDY.
And amidst such a state of things can my friend Vladimir manage to exist? — he, the hero of one of the most delicious adventures.

OSIPP (*ironically*).
Aha! we understand — Lydia!

HARDY (*not understanding*).
Lydia! Lydia! To the best of my knowledge her name was Katinka.

IVAN.
And was formerly called Lydia. Incomprehensible!

VASIL.
I find it very comprehensible. One is called Lydia; the other, Katinka!

OSIPP.
So Katinka is another?

VLADIMIR (*bashfully*).
Yes: Katinka is another.

ALL (*merrily*).
Long live Katinka!

VASIL.
Well, I should say you have made good use of your time! What was it about Katinka? Out with it!

HARDY (*relating*).
Katinka is the young wife of an aged diplomat. One day —

VLADIMIR (*interrupting*).
I must protect the lady from journalistic malice. One day she wrote to me [*cites the letter*]. "My husband is going to London; I, to our estate in the Caucasus. My companion is ill, and unable to go with me. Her position is not yet filled. I know

a person whom I regard as adapted to the place. Will this person have the courage and love to share my loneliness with me?"

VASIL.
Ah! I understand. By this person —

VLADIMIR.
I was meant! I did not need a second hint, but donned feminine attire; was presented to the servants as Fatinitza, the new companion, and undertook the journey with the countess. On the evening of our arrival a carriage rattled into the courtyard, and out of a tenfold fur cloak was unwrapped —

VASIL.
Holy Petrovitch! the husband!

VLADIMIR.
No! his brother, — an officer of high degree in the army, a uniformed polar bear in the rough, — who surprised us with the announcement of a long visit. To behold me, and to fall mortally in love with me, was the work of a moment with him.

VASIL.
Then you must have looked devilish handsome as a girl.

VLADIMIR.
So said the Polar Bear! He followed me as if demented. Fearful of discovery, I was compelled to flee. Fatinitza became Lieut. Vladimir again. Such, comrades, was the end of the adventure with Katinka.

VASIL.
What? The lad knows such stories as this, and keeps them to himself all this while! For shame, comrade! Why, garnished with all its details, this story might have whiled away an hour or so of our ennui here in camp.

HARDY.
The deuce! why don't you do as the French used to do in the Crimea, and improvise a theatre in camp?

IVAN.
That would be sport!

ALL.
Wouldn't it?

VASIL.
A theatre without ladies!

HARDY.
Why, do you imagine the French used to have a tragedienne and a comical old woman detailed to every company? And, why, here we have the fair Fatinitza!

ALL.
Hurrah! So we have! Bravo! Now let us set about it!

VASIL.
What! we get up such mummeries?

ALL.
Yes, captain, we are so fearfully bored.

VASIL.
Well, then, go ahead.

ALL.
Bravo! Hurrah!

VLADIMIR.
But what shall we play?

HARDY.
I can help you out with that.

OSIPP.
I'll wager he has a whole theatre *repertoire* in his bag, — at least a comedy.

HARDY.
You've guessed it. [*Takes a pamphlet from his bag.*]

VASIL.
Queer provender.

HARDY.
Mere accident. A young dramatist presented me with a copy of his tragedy in one act, "The Treacherous Postal Card; or, The Letter-Carrier's Revenge!"

VLADIMIR.
A tragedy?

HARDY.
No comedy ever made me laugh so heartily as this tragedy. Now to work!

VLADIMIR.
And I, — the leading lady, — what shall I wear?

VASIL.
An old soldier's cloak and the cook's apron!

VLADIMIR.
Oh, my feminine vanity could not stand that!

STEIPANN.
I know just what you want. The soldiers found a Wallachian peasant-girl's entire Sunday outfit in a deserted hut last week.

HARDY.
Good enough! So we can have our first fulldress rehearsal to-day; to-morrow the performance in the light of a dazzling snow illumination. A critical æsthetical notice of the same in the next "Herald."

OSIPP.
I hope you will not take us down too hard.

(*Exit of* CADETS.)

JULIAN.
Easy to find those whose wits are straying—
But thus the journalist is never caught.
 Merry and steady,
 Witty and ready,
Frank, and with pleasant humor fraught.

CHORUS.
Now, to work! we must no more delay;
There's much to do to-day.

JULIAN.
 To labor now!
 Well, then, shalt thou
First actor be;
The tyrant, he!
The leader's part for me.

STEIPANN.
The prompter here you see.

VASIL.
The old man I will be.

FEDOR.
I'll sing the tenor high.

IVAN.
In choruses sing I.

OSIPP.
And I'll the villain try.
So good bye; we're off now.

STEIPANN.
We must no more delay—
There's much to do to-day!
The parts we've yet to con,
The dresses to try on—

CHORUS.
Now to work let us haste—
No more time must we waste.
What a pleasant thought!
A grand success will soon be wrought.
So, good bye; we go now
To devise—to arrange—to prepare!
  JULIAN.
And if an orchestra should fail us—
  CHORUS.
Tschin, ta, ta, ra, ta!
Our drum and trumpet will avail us—
Tschin, ta, ta, ra, ta!
  JULIAN.
And he who don't applaud with zeal,
Of bread and water be his meal!
  CHORUS.
Tschin, boom, &c.
We are sure to succeed!
  JULIAN AND CHORUS.
And for this the whole troupe in **accord**
Are licensed to applaud.

(*As foregoing.*)

STEIPANN (*alone*).
So I am to write off the parts in this cold!
Brrr! I must fire up first. [*Drinks.*] So then!
[*Seats himself.*] How shall I begin? [*Reads*]
" Scene first. Susanna alone. She sits on a sofa
bathed in tears — wet handkerchief "— if she
doesn't get the rheumatics! [*Reads*] " Loud. Here
I have the portrait of my husband!" [*Speaks*]
Ah, yes! It says *loud* — so it must be this way
[*yells*] " Here I have the portrait of my husband!"
[*Reads*] " As." [*Speaks*] A. S., A. S., what
in the deuce does that mean ? — A. S. At
Schnapps, perhaps. Yes, yes! at Schnapps. Most
natural thing in the world : the husband is at his
schnapps. [*Writes*] " My husband at his schnapps."
[*Reads*] " The more I see of my husband, the
better I like my lover!" [*Laughs*] Ha, ha, ha!
Pretty good! Brrr! How cold! Must fire up again.
[*Takes his canteen.*] What? empty so quick ?
Well, I must go and draw on my reserves. [*Rises.*]
Husband at his schnapps! Ha, ha, ha! [*Exit.*]

KANTCHUKOFF (*enters*).

GENERAL'S SONG.
Thousand fifes! and drums and cannon!
Where are all the guards on duty ?
Base paltroons, these dragoons!
I'll scratch their hides and spoil their beauty,
I'll scratch their hides and spoil their beauty,
To set them shaking and loud howls making.
    I know how!
  I'm general here!
    Kantchukoff!
  I'm general here!
    Kantchukoff!
Brave and skilful in commanding
Both Tartars and Cossacks,
And how to manage understanding
  Mon-go-lians and Mujaks!
  Finns and Russians,
  Turcomanians,
  Sam-oi-des
  And Lith-u-anians,
  Greeks, Kamschatkans,

Letts and Druses,
Lapps, Bulgarians, and Tunguses, —
Every regiment in line I keep
With this good whip, — Fst! fst!
  Ah, yes! I lash them!
Fst! Ah, yes, I lash them, fst!
Upon their backs with my own hand
  I thrash them!
With this I lash them. Fst! ah!
Yes. I lash them, fst!
A brave commander is the valiant chief,
  Kantchukoff!
    II.
From one fault a thousand springing
  Admits no dissension;
But to complaints each one is bringing
  I pay no attention.
Better argue without mincing
By this instrument convincing;
Spur the lazy, laggards moving,
Talents wake to seek improving.
Every regiment in line I keep, &c.

STEIPANN (*returns, sees the general — is startled*).
Good Lord! The general of the division!
[*About to slink away.*]

GENERAL (*severely*).
Halt!
  STEIPANN (*trembling*).
General!
  GENERAL.
Knave, you tremble! I see you know me! Who
are you, soul of a dog?

STEIPANN.
Sergeant Steipann, secretary of the company.

GENERAL.
Your papers!
  STEIPANN.
Here, general!

GENERAL (*looks over papers*).
Forage certificates — Roster — good! [*Returns all
the papers but one.*]

STEIPANN (*more courageously*).
Good clear writing, isn't it, general?

GENERAL (*reads*).
" Here I have the portrait of my husband at his
schnapps. [*Growling as he reads.*] So much the
more I like my lover!" By the beard of St. Peter,
what is all that devilish nonsense?

STEIPANN.
General!
  GENERAL.
Adjutant!
  ADJUTANT.
General!
  GENERAL.
One hundred lashes with the knout for this
scoundrel!
  STEIPANN.
Mercy, general!
  GENERAL.
Hold your jaw! I'll show you a husband at his
schnapps!

HARDY (*enters from barracks. Aside, referring to
  VLADIMIR'S disguise*).
That will make some jolly sport.

GENERAL.
And here? A civilian? A spy?
[*Seizes* HARDY *by the collar, and slings him towards adjutant.*]
Two hundred lashes!

HARDY.
Beg pardon! I am—

GENERAL.
I don't care a candle what you are. First the knout, and then the explanation.

HARDY.
Oho! quite the contrary! Here is my passport!

GENERAL.
Countersigned by the Grand Duke! Very well! But this rascal here (*pointing to* STEIPANN)—the knout!

STEIPANN.
General!

GENERAL.
One hundred lashes, correctly counted!

STEIPANN.
Mercy! mercy! [*Adjutant exit, with* STEIPANN *dragged by two Cossacks.*]

HARDY (*aside*).
One hundred lashes! Horrible! I must tell Vladimir and his comrades who has come!

GENERAL.
Halt!

HARDY.
Whom have I the honor of obeying?

GENERAL.
I am Count Timofey Kantchukoff, commanding-general of this division! And you—

HARDY.
I? A newspaper correspondent.

GENERAL.
A newspaper correspondent? [*Returns the passport contemptuously.*] Bah! I have often wondered what you fellows were made for. I suppose you are all only around to betray our movements.

HARDY.
Movements? The army hasn't moved for three months!

GENERAL.
You herald our defeats to all quarters of the world.

HARDY.
We would have been glad to have heralded some victories; but—

GENERAL.
You exaggerate our losses.

HARDY.
Ah, general! what would be thought of the strength of your army if we hadn't?

GENERAL.
All the same. I can't use any newspaper man here at the front. You will please walk back to Bucharest between two Cossacks.

HARDY.
But, general!—

GENERAL.
I don't want the slightest blunder I make telegraphed all over the world.

HARDY.
Then make no blunders!

GENERAL.
Now, what do you know about strategy?

HARDY.
Not much of that kind. But I understand what blunders are, and make my living by blaming them. But strategic blunders are not the worst a person can make, general.

GENERAL.
Ah!

HARDY (*aside*).
Now may all my eloquence help me! He must let up on the poor sergeant. [*Aloud*] My frosty friend, I read in these weather-beaten features, that, in spite of your rough exterior, you have a warm and humane heart.

GENERAL (*dumbfounded—aside*).
Can he read my love for Fatinitza in my nose?

HARDY (*aside*).
And, if I can beg off fifty lashes, it will be something. [*Aloud*] Therefore, general, I appeal to your heart.

GENERAL.
We are all human. Every one has his sensitive spot.

HARDY.
Sergeants too, haven't they?

GENERAL.
Sergeants and generals. I have experienced it myself.

HARDY.
What! [*aside*] he too?

GENERAL.
Once in my life!

HARDY (*aside*).
Oh these Russians!

GENERAL.
But I feel it still!

HARDY (*aside*).
Well that knout must have cut pretty deep!

GENERAL.
She was my first and only love!

HARDY.
Love? [*aside*] and I thought—[*gesture of lashing*]—the knout!

GENERAL.
I loved her,—and she reciprocated! [*Violently*] Yes, sir, she reciprocated!

HARDY.
I have not the slightest disposition to doubt it.

GENERAL.
My happiness lasted but a few days. She disappeared, and since then I have been vainly striving to find her.

VLADIMIR (*at this moment enters from barracks, disguised in becoming Wallachian peasant-girl's costume*).
Here I am at last!

GENERAL.
Chorrt vasmi!! Fatinitza! Speak of angels, and they appear.

VLADIMIR.
O Lord!—the Polar Bear!

HARDY (*aside*).
He the Polar Bear! The bombshell has burst!

14   FATINITZA.

GENERAL.
What, Fatinitza, idol of my heart! you here — in this costume?

VLADIMIR.
Yes — I —

HARDY (*quickly*).
The young lady came to see her brother, Lieut. Vladimir. She donned this costume that she might ourney with greater security.

GENERAL.
Her brother? Where is this brother?

VLADIMIR.
He is — he was —

HARDY.
The Turks attempted a surprise yesterday, and Lieut. Vladimir was captured after a heroic resistance.

GENERAL.
The Vladimir shall be rewarded!

HARDY.
His sister brought ransom money! That's what I call imagination!

VASIL (*enters very merrily from barracks with* OSIPP).
I look gloriously in these clothes! Dearest niece!

GENERAL.
Chorrt vasmi! You infernal hound!

VASIL.
Great guns, the general! [*Runs back.*] Company, to arms!

SENTRIES (*call*).
To arms! to arms!

VASIL.
Attention, company! Present arms!

GENERAL.
Chorrt vasmi! Hound of a captain! This will cost you your command!

STEIPANN (*enters*.)
Help! help! O general! Mercy! mercy!

ADJUTANT.
The general ordered one hundred lashes!

GENERAL.
One hundred? Three hundred! Five hundred! And every tenth man in the company one thousand!

HARDY.
He is strong in his decimals!

ADJUTANT.
As you command, general.

HARDY.
Fatinitza must help us now!

VLADIMIR.
I understand!

DUETTINO.

VLADIMIR.
If she with true heart, loves me so dearly
  Hope I sincerely she'll pardon all;
  All that love tender claims, love will render—
  Love knows not how to deny love's call.
  Here I'll stay no longer pouting,
  Frowning sullenly and doubting,
  If you just smile a little:
  Smile now, do!

GENERAL.
Ha! ha ha!

VLADIMIR.
Ah, laugh a little more!
  Wilt laugh or not more gaily?
  Ah, faces that are stern give no delight:
  Only those that laugh can please the rig' '
  Laugh once more, a tiny laugh! a little more!
  Now laugh again, now do! more, more!
  Bravo! bravo! I'm not so cruel as before '

GENERAL.
Ha! ha! ha! ha!

VLADIMIR.
Hearts that have feeling cruel are never :
  My prayers will ever find grace anew.
  "Honey is sweeter, drawn from flowers bitter,"
  So says the proverb, and, faith, 'tis true!
  Here I'll stay no longer pouting, &c.

GENERAL.
Well, then, for the first time in my life I will let mercy temper justice [*in undertone*] for your sake, Fatinitza. [*Aloud*] But there must be some punishment. [*He sneezes.*]

THE ENTIRE COMPANY (*in concert*).
Saluto, general!

GENERAL.
Bless you, my children! Captain, company drill for two hours. [*In undertone*] That's how I get them out of the way.

VASIL. Company, right face! March!

CHORUS. When in robes of white, &c.

GENERAL.
I shall soon be at hand to witness your manœuvres.

VASIL.
At your command, general.

GENERAL.
Now, get out of this!

VASIL.
Company, right face! March!

HARDY.
I must make a first-class special out of that! What a pity I can't sketch!

VLADIMIR (*aside*).
It is now high time for Fatinitza to disappear, and for Lieut. Vladimir to come on to the scene. [*Going.*]

GENERAL.
Fatinitza, at last we are alone together! Idol of my heart! come, come. And now let me press the first sweet kiss of our meeting upon your maiden lips.

VLADIMIR.
Heavens! [*Aside*] and I have just been drinking allash!

GENERAL.
The same shy, coy creature of old! Just one kiss, only one kiss, Fatinitza!

VLADIMIR.
On my forehead, general.

GENERAL.
Call me Timofey.

VLADIMIR.
On my forehead, Timofey.

GENERAL.
What a fool I would be!

VLADIMIR.
Ha! monster!

FATINITZA.
WHEN IN ROBES OF WHITE.

FATINITZA. 17

GENERAL.
Oh, balsam, ambrosia, nectar!

VLADIMIR (aside).
He doesn't say a word about alash.

GENERAL.
Listen, beloved maiden: I will gain a sacred right unto thee. This ring, it shall seal our union. [Producing a ring.]

VLADIMIR.
I dare not take it.

GENERAL (passionately).
You must! you must! [He forces the ring on to his finger.] So, so! Now you are mine for life, my betrothed, soon my wife!

VLADIMIR.
His wife! Chorrt vasmi! That is the first offer of marriage I ever had.

GENERAL.
So much the better! so much the better!

VLADIMIR (aside).
How shall I save myself? [Aloud as before] But, general—

GENERAL.
Call me Timofey, affianced, husband; and take this kiss of betrothal—

VLADIMIR.
On my hand, on my hand, Timofey!

GENERAL.
Ah, demnition! A kiss of betrothal on the hand! On the mouth, the mouth!

HARDY (rushing on).
General, general!

GENERAL.
Chorrt vasmi! Who dares disturb me?

HARDY.
I, general, with permission!

VLADIMIR (aside).
Somebody at last!

GENERAL.
What is it?

HARDY.
General, I have to announce that a splendid sleigh is coming this way!

GENERAL.
What's that to me?

HARDY.
A glance with my field-glass discovered a handsome young lady in the sleigh.

GENERAL.
A lady! Holy Petrovitch! my niece! I had forgotten her entirely. The girl has her head filled with fantastic notions. She wants to see the war for herself; but she will be sent to a convent at once. What has the Princess Lydia Imanovna to do in camp?

VLADIMIR (startled, aside).
Lydia! Heavens! [Aloud] General!

GENERAL (tenderly).
Call me Timofey!

VLADIMIR.
Timofey, what is the name of your niece?

GENERAL (with vexation).
Lydia Imanovna. The deuce take her!

VLADIMIR.
Heavens! what shall I do? It's all up with me now, my dear fellow.

HARDY.
Why?

VLADIMIR.
I love Lydia Imanovna. She is the cause of my having been transferred to this place. She will recognize me. What shall I do?

HARDY.
Don't worry, my boy: I will rescue you.

SLEIGHING SONG.

LYDIA (not seeing VLADIMIR & JULIAN).
At head-quarters, dearest uncle,
I arrive with eager longing,
To behold upon the field itself,
The proofs of valor bright.

GENERAL.
Buried here, 'mid snow-drifts frightful,
What you wish, pray now confide.

LYDIA.
Oh! a sleigh-ride is delightful,
And romantic, too, beside!
What delight, within a light sleigh seated—
Onward bounding!
And to hear the tinkling bells in measure
Gaily sounding!
To sweep and sway,
Like zephyrs at their play—
  So light! So bright!
Thus young love flies away!
To sweep and sway,
Like winds at play;
Thus, like a breath, we dash away.

VLADIMIR.
'Tis she! What delight my heart doth fill!
I seem to dream—am I truely waking still?

JULIAN & GENERAL.
So light! so bright! o'er the smooth and icy way
To sweep and sway, like zephyrs at their play!

LYDIA.
Safe and warm, by robes of fur protected,
All fret and care are from my thoughts rejected.
  Forms now in sight
  Swiftly take flight.
Ah! often times thus disappear
Dreams that to the heart were dear!
Ah, 'tis vain! thus recalling
Visions vanished! To-day,
Hence! Away—
Such thoughts enthralling!
Coursers light, speed away!
  What delight, &c.

VLADIMIR.
Ah! what delight, in rapid flight
To glide and dash,
Like the lightning's flash!
So near to me, her do I see.
Vision lovely! Love's brightest dream!

JULIAN & GENERAL.
Ah! what delight, in rapid flight
To glide and dash
Like the lightning's flash! dzin, &c.
The bells are sounding,
The gay steeds bounding.

FATINITZA.

QUARTETTE.

GENERAL.
There's a cloister near the field,
That to you will shelter yield.

LYDIA.
In a cloister you'd confine me,
Your exploits from me concealing,
While I here may safely stand
And see all close at hand!

GENERAL.
Would it in you becoming be
To stay here unprotected?
Hast on the risks reflected—
Of what may chance to thee?
And, therefore, as I plainly see
How dull would be such dwelling—
This gentle dame, if willing,
Shall thy companion be.

VLADIMIR.
Oh, heaven! Alas!

LYDIA (*taken aback.*)
This young lady?

GENERAL.
Yes: this lady!

LYDIA.
What do I see?

GENERAL.
This, now, is fine!

LYDIA.
This lady fair—the truth to tell—
With wonder makes me tremble;
So much doth she resemble
A youth I once knew well!

VLADIMIR (*joyfully*).
To whom you courtesy did show
That aided and relieved him;
Perhaps, you have believed him
Forgetful—'tis not so.

ALL FOUR.
I must, in truth, confess
'Tis a peculiar case.
The fact absurd doth seem—
I think 'tis all a dream!
But this affair in hand,
I cannot understand.

LYDIA.
And do you know the youth I mention?

VLADIMIR.
Yes, surely; he my brother is!

JULIAN.
She is his sister!

LYDIA.
'Tis surprising!

JULIAN.
And to this sister he is twin!

LYDIA.
Where, at present, is your brother?

VLADIMIR.
They made him prisoner, yesterday.

JULIAN.
To ransom him she came this way!

LYDIA.
For him we will united pray.

JULIAN.
Their prayers together they will say!
If he, disguised as maid, was taken,
Fortunate the captor is!

GENERAL.
To-day, 'tis late already
At the cloister to instate you;
We must accomodate you
For well, or ill, with us!
Meanwhile, as at my quarters
Many may be standing by
Yet in here (*pointing to barrack*) you may [quie
And rest you without fuss!

LYD., VLA. & JUL.
Ah!

GENERAL.
The place is small for two;

LYDIA.
What now——

VLADIMIR.
Oh, heaven——

JULIAN.
Now, joy——

GENERAL.
But you can make it do.

LYDIA.
will happen!

VLADIMIR.
I think so!

JULIAN.
be with you.

GENERAL.
Though narrow is the space,
You'll find room to embrace! Come on!
All right now, and keep up good heart!

LYDIA & VLADIMIR.
Oh, yes, that is true;
I will with all my heart.

JULIAN.
He in a nice, warm nest will hide,
While I am freezing here outside!

ALL FOUR.
All is right! All is right!

LYDIA.
Such resemblance near,
Doth most strange appear:
Wavering doubts o'erflood the soul
  With stupor dull.
In that glance, now shineth bright
The tender flame that doth my heart relight
Sweet enchantment, here beside him!
  Fly not away!

If 'tis a dream, I would not wake again.
    Doth he control my heart
      With spells enchaining?
    Or does desire mislead—
      His presence feigning?
    Ah, no! fly not away.
If 'tis a dream, I would not wake again,
    If 'tis a dream, &c.

VLADIMIR.

Such resemblance near
Doth most strange appear!
A stupor doubt o'erflows the soul.
In that glance, I see, doth shine
The tender flame that lights up mine.
    That doth my heart relight!
    'Tis she that wins my heart
      With her enchantment!
    Or does desire mislead—
      Her presence feigning?
Oh, image fair! ah, do not fly away!
If I dream, let me not wake again!
    Doth she control my heart
      With spells enchaining?
    Or does desire mislead—
      Her presence feigning?

JULIAN.

Oh, what a brilliant item waits,
    Insertion by my journal!
"Within a convent's quiet gates,
    An officer supernal,
Will teach the monks to march in line
    And how to drill
In arms with handy skill.
A fair battalion feminine
Perhaps he'll raise at will,
And put them through the drill."

GENERAL.

This plan now consummated,
And appetites well sated,
No more I'll leave; don't fear,
No one can molest you here.

[*At the close of this quartet, the General retires toward the background, meanwhile making threatening gestures in the direction where the soldiers are supposed to be drilling. He calls out.*]

GENERAL.

Quicker! livelier, there, you infernal rascals! One! two!—left! right! (*Exit both*, R.)
(VLA. *conducts* LYDIA *towards first barrack*, L.)

JULIAN (*catches his arm*).
Miss Fatinitza must not forget her brother.

VLADIMIR (*indignantly*).
Be assured; my respect for Lydia is equal to my love. (*Exit both*.)

JULIAN.
However it be (*steps to entrance of barracks*), it is better that I should remain at hand. (*Aloud.*) The ladies will excuse me: I have left some of my luggage in there. (*Enters hut, taking off hat and closing door behind him.* VUIKA *has entered from* R. *as* VLADIMIR *makes his exit with* LYDIA.)

FINALE.

(VUIKA, *on seeing the stage deserted gives a signal toward* R., *and* HASSAN BEY *appears with a wild band of Bashi-Bazouks, who come forward cautiously. Several noiselessly overpower the sentries, who are looking with curiosity off* R. *at the Russians drilling. Others spike the cannon, and throw down the Russian flagstaff.*)

CHORUS OF BASHI-BAZOUKS.

Now up, away!
    No sound betray
To warn them of the rage impending;
    Be watchful, keen,
    Let naught be seen;
They can't escape their doom impending.
    If bold in deed,
    We must succeed,
And naught allow to fail at need!

Bashi-Bazouks, if to your skill
Shall fate accord its favors still,
With booty laden you'll return,
And sing in triumph all you earn.
    Yok, yok, yok, yok, tra, la, la, ra, la, &c.
The grandest booty of the war!
    La, la, la, la, la, la, la.

Light of foot, on we go,
To conceal our raid impending,
    Silent, slow! forward, now!
No escape for them we'll show:
No chance for them we'll show!
    Yok, yok, yok, yok, tra, la, la, ra, la.
The grandest booty of war!
    La, la, la, la, la, la, la.

Now, on! away!
Soft, soft, no sound betray!
Soft, soft! if brave in deed,
    We must succeed!

HASSAN.
(*Who, led by* VUIKA, *has crept to the barrack.*)
There are three in here!

(CHORUS *drag* VLADIMIR, JULIAN, *and* LYDIA *out of the hut.* JULIAN *cries out.* HASSAN *presents a revolver.*)

CHORUS.
They are ours! They're ours!
As pris'ners we'll secure them!

VLADIMIR (*who has snatched a sword*).
You must o'erthrow and slay me,
Ere her you take from me!

CHORUS.
A maid in arms!
Was ere such fun—
Ah, ha, ha, ha, ha!
Beneath the sun!

VLADIMIR.
Leave her alone!

CHORUS.
Ha, ha, ha, ha, ha!

VLADIMIR.
Ah, help—some one!

JULIAN.
A case to be worked up is here—
An article will soon appear.

CHORUS.
It makes me laugh! Ah! ha, ha, ha! Such fun!
No arm has power to wrest you now from me.
Resist no more; as prisoners now surrender.
Vain are prayers, and vain your threats will be.
  The victors brave
  Will you enslave—
  Then quickly yield;
  Your prayers are vain!
  We the victory gain!

VLADIMIR & LYDIA.
Valor brave and bold!
You robbers, hold!
No, no !
I ne'er to you will her surrender!
While I still may,
Will I resist your sway!
Yes, yes, yes, yes!
I shall resist, resist your sway.
Yes, in my breast the fury raging
Finds relief, itself assuaging.
You are all as outlaws banded;
Soldiers? No! but traitors branded!
Yes, all your fire
Will soon expire,
When 'neath the flag of our soldiers so brave,
The victor comes, our lives to save.
When 'neath the flag, &c.
You're a band of thieving knaves;
Soldiers not, but trait'rous slaves!
Yes, you are trait'rous slaves.

JULIAN (*producing note-book*).
I'll now begin (*writing*).
An officer of jovial of part,
Investing in a maiden's heart,
And wounded sore by Cupid's dart,—
He thought the cloister he would gain,
And with the fair one there remain.
They strolled together towards the gate,
When on the way—thro' cruel fate—
  Just like a flash
  From cloudless sky,
  The Turks did dash
On them, and took them on the sly!
Shots followed fast behind, like hail,
'Mid cries and howls without avail!
Regiments of friends at last appear;
  A general fight
  Took place at sight;
Of which I here results will write :
Of Turks, a thousand bit the dust,
While we but one brave man have lost.

HASSAN (*points to* JULIAN).
You may buy again
Those dames with price of gold;
As mediator bold
You'll here remain.
JULIAN. Your humble servant!
HASSAN. Six thousand roubles is the price —
JULIAN. That's not outrageous!
HASSAN. Or in gold sequins—we're not nice!
JULIAN. With greatest pleasure!
HASSAN. And good or bad, make no delay.
JULIAN. No doubts admitted!
HASSAN. Lest they should at the Harem stay.

LYDIA, VLADIMIR & JULIAN. Alas!
CHORUS OF BULGARIANS. Oh, heaven!
CHORUS. Ha, ha!
LYDIA & VLADIMIR. Despair!
JULIAN 'Tis bad!
CHO. OF BULGARIANS. What's this?
CHORUS. That's good!
LYDIA & VLADIMIR.
All hope of aid is banished now!
Prisoners here we remain,
Freedom we shall ne'er regain!
Where is he? where can he be?
With his band why tarries he?
Ah! where is he, where can he be?
Cowards! Traitors! Robbers! Ah!

JULIAN.
There's naught to say, and naught to do!
Prisoners here they remain;
Freedom they shall ne'er regain.
Where is he, where can be
Kantschukoff? why tarries he?
Farewell, cloister harum-scarum;
Thou art changed into a Harem;
Inmates turned, *sans* leave or law,
To Odalisques for some Bashaw.
Here a moral I will draw, pyramidal,
Or in a dream, sanguine, raw, a grand final.

CHORUS OF BULGARIANS.
Pris'ners here they remain,
Freedom they shall ne'er regain.
Where is he, where can he be,
With his band why tarries he?
Where can he be, where does he stay?
The soldier brave, why tarries he?
Quickly, promptly, off—away!

HASSAN & CHORUS.
Your hope is vain!
As prisoners you'll remain, I maintain.
He who'd save you's far away.
Where is he? where can he be?
With his band why tarries he?
Where can he lay? I will not stay;
We weary longer here to stay.
No more delay; we will not stay;
We're weary now of this delay.

VUIKA (*enters*). The Russians are coming!
HASSAN. Quick! To the Harem!

JULIAN.
(*Is at extreme* R., *and is prevented from calling Russians by a gigantic Bashi-Bazouk, who keeps him back with his rifle. As this Bashi-Bazouk withdraws towards* R. JULIAN *advances; as soon as the Turk disappears,* JULIAN *leaps on to a gun carriage, and calls*) Help!

GENERAL.
(*Enters* L. *with Russian Soldiers. A few of these leap on the ramparts, and fire after the Turks.*) Halt there! You might hit Fatinitza!

(VASIL *raises the prostrate Russian standard again.* GEN. KANTSCHUKOFF *falls half helpless into* JULIAN'S *arms, and the latter rests his note-book on the general's back and writes furiously. Tableau. Snow begins to fall.* CURTAIN.)

END OF FIRST ACT.

SECOND ACT.

"KISMET."

The Harem of Izzet Pasha in the Fortress of Rustchuk.

INTRODUCTION.

NURSIDAH. BESIKA. DIONA. ZULEIKA. SLAVES.

To the native fascinations
Of a face that's fair and charming,
Novel graces art doth add with lavish hand,
All to please the lover's eye;
These unfold at his command
Every charm, languish and sigh.
La, la, la! coquetting with soft addresses,
  And fond caresses,
Each seductive charm we try.

NURSIDAH.
Upon the shoulders,
Powders soft enhance their whiteness.
SLAVES. (*Alti*.) They are here.
DIONA.
While on the cheeks, the roses
Sometimes need reviving.
SLAVES. (*2d Sop*.) With this—
BESIKA.
I'd tinge the lids, to give
The eyes more fire and brightness.
SLAVES. (*2d Alti*.) That's well!
ZULEIKA. Reach me the powders white!
SLAVES. (*2d Sop*.) They're here.
NURSIDAH. The carmine hand to me.
SLAVES. (*2d Alti*.) Ah, well!
DIONA. Where can the black dye be?
SLAVES. (*2d Sop*.) 'Tis here!
BESIKA. Bring perfumed waters light.
SLAVES. Yes.
ZULEIKA. The powders white.
SLAVES. Here.
NURSIDAH. The carmine here.
SLAVES. Yes.
DIONA. The black is near?
SLAVES. Here.
BESIKA. The odors light!

ENSEMBLE.
Odalisque, 'mid charms install thee,
Soon thy lord may deign to call thee.
To the native fascinations, &c.

MUSTAPHA.
What! still prinking? Hurry now! His highness is coming!
THE WOMEN. Izzet Pash? Ah!
MUSTAPHA. Here he is already.

ZULEIKA.
Let me kiss thine eyes, O lord and master!
THE OTHERS. Me too! Me too!

IZZET.
Come, let up! Whose turn is it to kiss me to-day?
ALL. Mine! Mine!

IZZET (*warding them off*).
Sabr! Sabr! (*meaning "patience."*) Order must be maintained—even in a harem! You know in principle I am opposed to the institution of a harem; but for the present I express my sentiments by giving all my kisses to *one* wife in each day. It won't do to bring on the reforms all in a lump, you see! So then who is the favored one to-day?

ZULEIKA (*approaches*).
I am, O lord and master. (*About to kiss him*.)

IZZET (*wards her off*).
Sabr! Allow me to verify! (*producing note-book, mutters*) Zuleika, Diona, Besika, Nursidah—Zuleika! Correct! (*Kisses* ZULEIKA.) Good morning, dear! The rest of you—get out of this!

THE OTHERS (*murmur*).
Oh!
IZZET (*emphatically*).
Or rather—no—stay and listen!

THE FOUR (*submissively*.)
To hear is to obey. We listen.

IZZET.
I have concluded to give you a new companion.

THE FOUR.
A fifth wife? Shame, shame!

IZZET.
But enough of this! My faithful Hassan Bey has captured two beautiful Christian maidens. He wishes to make me a present of them; and I can hardly refuse him and be consistent, since the re-reform party in Turkey is friendly to the Christians. I believe a man cannot show his regard for ladies better than by marrying them,—whether polygamously or monogamously is immaterial to me!

ALL (*indignantly*).
For shame!

IZZET.
Silence! I am friendly to the Christians, and in my own peculiar way give expression to the prevalent reformatory ideas — by reforming my harem.

WHEN SICK MEN ARE FAILING.

IZZET PASHA.

When sick men are failing,
  And growing more ill,
Strong measures to save them
  Must be used with skill.
To lie on soft lounges
  From morning till night,
Will fail to restore them,
  And bring them all right!
If a doctor is called in,
  Their ills to dispel,
He'll order waking, and he'll order shaking,
  To make them get well.

O Bosphorous charming!
  Thou'rt badly deranged,
Thy shores to a hospital
  Seem to me changed.
Thy treasury's empty,
  And loans would be vain;
Thy last operation
  Still causes thee pain!
If a doctor is called in
  Thy ills to dispel,
He'll order waking, and he'll order shaking,
  To make thee get well.

WHEN SICK MEN ARE FAILING.

When sick men are fail-ing, And grow-ing more ill, Strong mea-sures to save them Must be used with skill. To lie on soft loun-ges, from morn-ing till night, Will fail to re-store them, And bring them all right. If a doc-tor is called in, Their ills to dis-pel, He'll or-der

ZULEIKA.

So our lord and master loves us no more?

IZZET.

Oh, yes! Of course I love you; but, instead of being quartered, you must hereafter share my heart in fifths or sixths. It is plenty large enough!

IZZET.

Oh, don't make such a fuss, ladies! It's practical reform I want.

ALL WOMEN.

For shame!

IZZET.

Sabr! Silence!

MUSTAPHA.

Exalted sir! Hassan Bey humbly begs admittance. He brings the Christian maidens.

THE WOMEN.

For shame!

IZZET.

Hold your tongues! Put down your veils, and wrap yourselves in your mantles; and, Mustapha, see that not a soul of them stirs: if they do, intimidate them. The flogging of women is antagonistic to reform principles; but in practice the institution has a strikingly persuasive power. I don't want the new-comers to receive a poor impression of my marital life at first sight. If one of them stirs, Mustapha, you know how to persuade them to keep quiet.

[VUIKA, HASSAN BEY, VLADIMIR as FATINITZA, LYDIA, and two Bashi-Bazouks enter.]

HASSAN.

Exalted sir, here are the two Christian maidens. May the sun of your favor shine upon them!

IZZET (to VLADIMIR, who stands so that IZZET cannot see LYDIA).

Stand aside, maiden, and let me see your companion. Allah, il Allah! what a charming vision! Fair stranger, and the rest of you, listen: you are my favorite, the chosen wife of my heart, — you, and no other

FOUR WOMEN.

The hussy! Misfortune shower down upon her! Away with her!

IZZET.

Mustapha!

MUSTAPHA.

Effendim?

IZZET.

Persuade them!

IZZET (to LYDIA).

Come, beloved one! share the place of honor with me, and reign over us all.

LYDIA.

Away!

VLADIMIR.

Your highness, Princess Lydia Imanovna is the niece of the Russian general commanding the forces across the Danube.

IZZET.

So much the better! I have been longing for a Russian general's niece in my harem for some time.

VLADIMIR.

You cannot refuse a handsome ransom for the princess.

IZZET.

Who can make me take it?

VLADIMIR.

International law.

IZZET.

International law? International law — to use an Occidental expression — is mere bosh!

LYDIA.

Oh, horrible!

VLADIMIR (in undertone).

Be calm, princess! be calm! We will trust in Russian valor to rescue us.

IZZET.

The Princess Lydia shall be my favorite from this day forth. [Searching in pocket.] Where is my pocket-handkerchief? She is weeping. Oh, yes! I forgot: it is in the wash! [Calls] Mustapha!

MUSTAPHA.
Effendim?

IZZET.
Lend me your handkerchief.

HASSAN (points to VUIKA).
Your highness, it was this man whose cunning led us to the Russians.

VUIKA.
Your most extremely exalted highness!

IZZET.
Very well: you shall be rewarded in a princely manner.

VUIKA.
O your highness! Gospod!

IZZET.
Let me finish. You shall be rewarded in a princely manner as soon as we receive our money from Stamboul! They are already owing us forty-two months' salary.

VUIKA.
But, Gospod, I am a poor man of low station.

IZZET.
And I am a poor man in high station: that is the only difference between us.

VUIKA.
Oh, Gospod!

IZZET (to MUSTAPHA).
Well, then, give the rascal ten shekels.

VUIKA (receives money from MUSTAPHA).
Ten shekels! Gospod, I am devoted to you for a lifetime; I — But he has given me only five!

IZZET.
That's all right. Everybody who has any thing to do with us Turks must be satisfied with fifty per cent, and consider themselves lucky to get that.

VUIKA.
Oh, these devilish shabby Moslems!

VLADIMIR (whispers to VUIKA).
The Russians pay what they promise.

VUIKA (as he is led away by two Bashi-Bazouks, aside).
Just wait, Pasha: I shall be revenged! [Exit.]

IZZET.
One thing more. The Muscovitish attire of my bride destroys the illusion. Mustapha, get the best of clothing and jewelry ready. [To VLADIMIR.] And you? what is your name?

VLADIMIR (quickly).
Vladi— [Correcting] Fatinitza, your highness!

IZZET.
Well, Fatinitza, in the mean while you can assist your mistress at her toilet, until these perturbed spirits here have calmed themselves. The rest of you now follow me, and listen to a half-hour's lecture on domestic economy! [All exit except VLADIMIR and LYDIA.]

DUETTO.

VLADIMIR.
I fear to think what is her destiny.
With dread and doubt
I think what will the ending be;
What will it be?

LYDIA.
I fear to think what fate shall be.
What is my destiny?
What will of all the ending be?
The case a serious look doth wear;
But I'm not ready to despair:
Amid so many griefs
Some joy doth still remain, —
One friend I shall retain!

VLADIMIR.
Now honor commands: thy lips unseal!
This love doth withstand: No, not yet reveal!
What shall I do or say?
Which shall I heed? which voice obey?

LYDIA.
Here are the gems, the robe, and veil,
Costly, charming. Wilt thou begin
My hair to smooth and dress?

VLADIMIR.
Break not, O heart! thy grief repress!

LYDIA.
Thy string of pearls becomes me well.
Wilt lend me your aid?

VLADIMIR.
With all my heart I'll be your maid.

LYDIA.
Let us begin!

VLADIMIR.
You are obeyed.

LYDIA.
But, ah! be careful what you do!
Ah, such trembling movements nothing will avail!
Her hand is all unskilled; 'tis plain
She knows not how: her efforts only fail;
She tries, but loses time in vain.
The cause of such a trembling hand
I cannot understand:
If she knows not the way,
I'll dress myself to-day.

VLADIMIR.
Such trembling movements nothing will avail, &c.

LYDIA.
Well, then, will you be so kind
As to lend me now your hand
To arrange this pretty garland on my hair?
Now tastefully these pearls arrange for me.

VLADIMIR.
Ah, she will drive me mad, I see!

LYDIA.
This diadem is rich and rare:
'Tis well! now, come! let's finish now! 'tis growing late.

VLADIMIR.
Yes, yes! I'm here, and will not make you wait.

LYDIA and VLADIMIR.
But, ah! be careful what you do!

No more, no more! I'm not with silence gifted.

LYDIA.
What's coming now? what would you say?

VLADIMIR.
I will the truth no more conceal.

LYDIA.
Explain — what would you say?

FATINITZA.

VLADIMIR.
Howe'er my future it may mould,
I have resolved it must be told!

LYDIA.
What mystery dost conceal?
Come, speak! the truth reveal.

VLADIMIR.
Fraternal love burns within me,
And inspires me to tell you here,
Pray I now for Vladimir.

LYDIA.
What is this mystery he will reveal to me?

VLADIMIR.
Who with love wastes away,
Asks that thy heart pity should sway;
He ne'er hath courage found to reveal his affection,
But hides the fire profound that he feels from detection.
If softly thy tender heart is waking,
To thoughts of love so true, ah, yes!
He will see it, he will know,
He will listen and will hear
If love should hope, not fear!
Look on him with pitying eye,
And do not a pardon to him deny, —
To him who such love doth on thee bestow, —
And that brother, that brother am I!

LYDIA.
Ah, what hear I?
I seem to dream,
And fear that all may not be true!
Is he with me?
What rapture in a thought so new!
I seem to dream!

VLADIMIR.
'Tis like a dream!
She's here with me!
Ah, yes! she's still with me!

BOTH.
Fate turns now kindly from sorrows past;
Hope beckons me on with a smile at last;
Sweet voices of faith from above
I hear softly whispering words of love:
The hour of sorrow's past,
And love doth smile at last.

VLADIMIR.
And may I hope then?

LYDIA.
Who asks for little may yet hope for more!

BOTH.
Voices whisper words of love.

[*At the close of duet,* LYDIA *exit.* VLADIMIR, *who has conducted* LYDIA *to door, stands a moment gazing after her. The four women enter softly.*]

NURSIDAH.
Come, sisters, we cannot allow our lord and master to take this Christian maiden as wife. Come, let us scratch out her eyes. Ah! Revenge! revenge!

THE THREE OTHERS.
Revenge! revenge!

VLADIMIR.
For heaven's sake, ladies, don't come to blows! You are beside yourselves with rage. I comprehend the situation, and sympathize with you.

NURSIDAH.
What, Christian maiden! you, too, hate your companion?

VLADIMIR.
Hate? Quite the contrary!

NURSIDAH.
Perhaps you would like to put yourself in her place.

VLADIMIR.
No, upon my honor! Hear me, charming playmates. A hundred thousand piasters shall be yours if you help to set us free, — her and me.

NURSIDAH.
A hundred thousand piasters!

DIONA.
And we would be rid of them both!

VLADIMIR.
But it must be soon — this very day. I give you my word of honor as an officer that you shall receive the money.

NURSIDAH.
Your word of honor as an officer?

VLADIMIR.
Quite right. The word of honor which an officer over yonder has given to me, — a Russian lieutenant.

NURSIDAH.
Whom you love?

VLADIMIR.
Unspeakably! He and I are one in body and soul!

NURSIDAH.
And he has many women in his harem?

VLADIMIR.
Unfortunately he has not. Occidental civilization stupidly forbids a cavalry officer driving such a charming four-in-hand as you before his chariot of life.

ZULEIKA.
But what shall we do?

VLADIMIR.
Find us some means of escape. As I have said, a hundred thousand piasters are yours.

NURSIDAH.
You can trust in me: I will save you.

ALL FOUR.
You can trust in all of us.

VLADIMIR.
Most glorious!

DIONA.
But can we trust in you?

VLADIMIR.
Upon my honor!

BESIKA.
Honor? You are a woman!

VLADIMIR.
Perhaps not so much as you think; and, if it will win your confidence, then listen! The Princess Lydia is worshipped by a young Russian!

ZULEIKA.
And this Russian, — where is he?

VLADIMIR.
Not far from here.

ALL. Where? where?
VLADIMIR. Will you swear to assist him?
ALL. We swear!
VLADIMIR. Well, then!

SEXTETTE.—VLADIMIR.

Well, then! So know—that young Russian—is
myself!
THE WOMEN. Ha! A man! a man! Is it true?
VLADIMIR (*aside*). They're all half crazed!
ALL FOUR. A man! A man! Is it true?
VLADIMIR. So much amazed!
ALL. With us he's jesting.
VLADIMIR. They're whispering.
ALL. You are untruthful.
VLADIMIR. And smiling.
ALL. It cannot be—no!

VLADIMIR.

Like startled doves, affrighted,
These women fly, excited,
If you breathe the name of man—
They go circling around in their flight,
But soon alight,
Recovered from their fright.

ALL FOUR.

We closely scan.
Is she a man?
What then are we? no! no!

NURSIDAH.

Thou a man? It cannot be!
Face and form say "no," you see.
Rosy cheeks, like those you wear—
Man ne'er boasted such a pair!
Rosy cheeks, like those you bear,
Men don't wear—no! Ha, ha, ha, &c.
Thou a man? It cannot be!

ALL FOUR.

Ha, ha, ha, ha, ha, ha, ha!
Thou a man? It cannot be!

DIONA.

Thou a man? No, say not so;
'Twould be falsehood, lies, you know.
Little feet, like those you own,
Are, thank heav'n, for us alone!
Little feet, like those you own,
Are ours alone, yes! Ha, ha, ha, &c.
Thou, a man? No, say not so!

ALL FOUR.

Ha, ha, ha, ha, ha, ha, ha! &c.

ZULEIKA.

Thou a man? No, 'tis not true;
Men could never laugh like you!
Merry glance, like that you throw,
Eye of man could never show!
Merry glance, like that you throw,
Men ne'er show, no! Ha, ha, ha! &c.
Thou a man? No, 'tis not true!

ALL FOUR.

Ha, ha, ha, ha, ha, ha, ha, &c.

BESIKA.

Thou a man? It makes me laugh!
Where do men have e'en the half
Such a charming mouth as this,
With such coral lips to kiss;
Such a charming mouth as this—
Made to kiss, no! Ha, ha, ha! &c.
Thou a man? It makes me laugh!

ALL FOUR.

Ha, ha, ha, ha, ha, ha, ha! Thou a man, &c.

VLADIMIR.

To many charms and graces
You are pleased to find in me;
Half those your fancy traces
Might well make me vain, you see!
You err; come touch me bravely,
Proof you'll find I'm not a Miss;
Then on each mouth I'll naively
Leave a kiss!

ALL FOUR.

Ah, yes! a kiss thus offered,
As a proof of sex may serve;
A young man's lips will swiftly
Send a thrill through every nerve!
So, if your lips are not like ice,
But like a bright flame burn,
That you're a young man, sweet and nice,
To doubt no more, we'll learn.

NURSIDAH & DIONA.

Come, kiss me now!

ZULEIKA & BESIKA.

Without delay.

ALL.

The riddle's key thou'lt quickly show
If thou art a man or no.

LYDIA.

(*Dressed in Turkish costume, enters hurriedly.*)
Hold up!

ALL FOUR (*angrily*).

I'd like to see what right has she
To thus prohibit this fair exhibit,
That goes forsooth, to show the truth—
Our mouths just missing the proffer'd kissing. Why?

LYDIA.

Because I have the right,
And he is greedy, quite.
Now cease this vain contention,
About a foolish flirt;
No kisses or caresses
Must you from me divert!

ALL FOUR.

If true, pray tell us why?

LYDIA.

I try to conceal in vain
The flame that within me is burning bright;
To him I devote all my love's sweet pain
Of this fond, and this only delight.

VLADIMIR.

O gentle heart, to thee
I'll ever faithful be;
Thou openest heaven to me,
More ask I not from thee.

VLADIMIR & LYDIA.

No more I ask or wish from thee,
Ever true to thee my heart shall be!

ALL FOUR.

We clearly see, no doubt remains;
From every claim we set you free.
A pledge of friendship, be this right hand!

LYDIA.

That heaven have pity, let us now demand

FATINITZA.

ALL.
When at evening, friendly shadows
Shroud the skies with their dark veil,
Then the work must be accomplished;
With strong hearts it cannot fail.
Keep on guard, with courage steeled,
Be our plans with care concealed,
So that nothing be revealed.
E'er the day is o'er
Shall freedom smile on us once more.

ZULEIKA (giving a key).
With this key unlock the wicket,
Of the cloister, near the thicket.

BESIKA.
Down the stairway, softly, mind you;
You will in the garden find you.

NURSIDAH.
Easy passage then you'll get
On the river, frozen yet.

ALL.
If the darkness us avail,
In our work we cannot fail;
Strong in heart, bold in deed,
In this work we'll succeed.

(*After the Sextette all exit. When the stage is empty* MUSTAPHA *enters and looks around.*)

MUSTAPHA.
Nobody here; so much the better. [*Calls out*] Bring in the Russian envoys!
[*Two officers enter, leading* HARDY *and* STEIPANN *blindfolded between them.*]

HARDY.
Ah! [*saluting*] Salem aleikum! Have the honor! What? nobody here?

STEIPANN.
Ah, Mr. Hardy! there is some kind of a Mussulman back there.

HARDY (*salutes several times*).
Effendi! salem aleikum! Allah, il Allah! Rahat lekum.

[MUSTAPHA *does not move.*]

HARDY.
My supply of Turkish is exhausted. Steipann, suppose you try.

STEIPANN.
I know only three Turkish words. *Bachi, pillaw,* and *bakshish*; that last meaning a fee. Suppose we try that. [*Bawls out*] Bakshish!
MUSTAPHA (*comes quickly forward with a servile salaam*).
Effendim?

HARDY.
The word "fee" has a wonderful effect in all languages. [*To* MUSTAPHA] Where is his excellency?

MUSTAPHA.
You will soon be permitted to sun yourselves in his presence!

HARDY (*to* MUSTAPHA).
And may I be permitted to ask in whose presence I am sunning myself at present?

MUSTAPHA.
I am Mustapha, guardian of the harem.

HARDY.
O fortunate man! So the care of the many better halves of his excellency is entrusted to you.

MUSTAPHA.
Evet! Yes!

VLADIMIR (*enters*).
His voice! It is he, with Steipann! Hardy, my dear old boy! how are you?

STEIPANN (*aside*).
Holy Petrovitch! the lieutenant!

MUSTAPHA (*swinging his whip*).
Allah kerim! Apart, apart! March in there, bold girl! or —

STEIPANN.
Beg pardon! but, my dear Kislar aga! —

MUSTAPHA.
Silence, Giaour! It would cost me my head if his excellency should learn that the sanctity of his harem had been violated.

HARDY (*presses a coin into his hand; leads him aside In undertone*).
Hush! Make no fuss about it. She is my sweetheart.

MUSTAPHA.
I understand.

VLADIMIR (*takes him aside. In undertone*).
Don't make any fuss about it: I am his sister.

MUSTAPHA.
Impossible!

STEIPANN (*as* VLADIMIR *and* HARDY *embrace once more, takes* MUSTAPHA *aside. In undertone*).
Let up a little, Moslem: she is his wife. [*Gives him money.*]

MUSTAPHA (*astonished*).
Allah kerim! His sister, his sweetheart, and the mother of his children. Oh these Muscovites!

VLADIMIR (*in undertone to* HARDY).
You come with ransom for Lydia and me. Hold Mustapha's attention for a moment: I want to speak a word with Steipann. [*Calls*] Steipann!

STEIPANN.
Lieutenant! — fairest Fatinitza, I meant to say.

HARDY (*approaches* MUSTAPHA; *takes him by the arm*).
We will leave them by themselves a moment, Effendi. He is her long-lost father!

MUSTAPHA.
Allah biller! What relations!

VLADIMIR (*has been with* STEIPANN *at background, where they have spoken animatedly together, and shown him the key secretly. In undertone*).
Here is the key.

STEIPANN.
I understand, lieutenant! I thought I would bring your uniform along, in case you wanted it.

MUSTAPHA.
Allah kerim! The Pacha is coming! Away, maiden! away to your chamber!

VLADIMIR.
I have told Steipann every thing. Now, try to send him back to our camp as soon as possible.

MUSTAPHA.
Away, or we are all lost!

VLADIMIR.
Now, take care, and be vigilant.

MUSTAPHA.
Off with you now, or we shall lose our heads!

[VLADIMIR *exit.* IZZET PASHA *appears in background.*]

MUSTAPHA.
The Russian envoys, your highness!

IZZET (*nods condescendingly*).
Kosh geldin! you are welcome! [*To* MUSTAPHA, *without turning his head*] Mustapha!

MUSTAPHA.
Effendim?

IZZET (*as before*).
Coffee! tobacco!

MUSTAPHA.
Kafédshi! Chibudshi!

IZZET.
You have come, O stranger, to offer me a ransom for one of my prisoners.

HARDY.
For both of them, your highness.

IZZET.
Then you will be disappointed. I shall retain the charming Lydia for myself. As for the other, she is nothing to me.

HARDY (*aside*).
So much the more to the general.

IZZET.
I will return her — in exchange for money, of course. Now, what do you offer for Fatinitza?

HARDY.
Ahem!

MUSTAPHA (*steals to* IZZET — *whispers quickly*).
Your highness, she is his wife.

IZZET (*aside*).
Then I will press him.

HARDY.
Well, your highness, I think a thousand rubles is plenty for her.

IZZET.
Oh, she is worth more than five times that sum!

HARDY.
Five thousand rubles? Your highness must be jesting. I will give two thousand.

IZZET.
Four thousand: those are bottom figures!

HARDY.
Then I guess we'll let you keep her, and welcome, your highness!

IZZET.
Allah, il Allah! I keep your wife?

HARDY.
She has a lot of faults: her greatest is a total lack of womanly qualities.

IZZET.
In spite of that she will cost you thirty-five hundred. But I will give up Lydia at no price. Her Kismét willed that she should fall to me, and she shall never have cause to regret it.

HARDY.
Kismét?

IZZET.
Yes, Kismét. — Mussulman for *fate.*

HARDY.
Ah, I understand!

IZZET.
We go it blind on Kismét.

HARDY.
Well, then, will your highness allow me to despatch this good man [*indicating* STEIPANN] with a letter to Count Kantchukoff, whom I must inform of your inexorable will?

IZZET.
You may. [*Calls as before*] Mustapha!

MUSTAPHA (*comes forward*).
Effendim?

IZZET (*in undertone*).
Have this man conducted with bandaged eyes as far as the river.

MUSTAPHA.
And the other?

IZZET.
Remains my guest.

HARDY (*writes. In undertone*).
Now, Steipann, tell the general six thousand men are not enough: we need twenty thousand.

STEIPANN.
All right, sir.

[MUSTAPHA *blindfolds him and leads him away.*]

IZZET.
Until the return of the Muscovite, O stranger! you shall partake of Izzet Pasha's hospitality. [*Claps his hands.*]

SERVANT (*enters*).
Effendim?

IZZET.
Champagne! [*Servant exit.*]

HARDY (*aside*).
Three claps of the hand mean champagne in Turkish. I must make a note of that! [*Aloud*] I had an idea that wine was forbidden to Mussulmans!

IZZET.
Champagne is no wine.

HARDY.
O veuve Cliquot! could you only hear that? [*Two servants bring two pails of ice with champagne-bottles, and also two very handsome beer-schooners.*]

HARDY.
What is champagne, then, if it is not wine?

IZZET.
Yellow soda-water.

HARDY (*looks wonderingly at the size of the glasses*).
Schooners! [*Drinks.*] Very good!

IZZET (*drinks; grows merrier*).
And if it were wine I wouldn't care a fig. I am a reform Turk! [*Drinks.*] Haha! reform is a good word! How do you like it, stranger?

HARDY.
First class, your highness; but I will no longer remain a stranger to you. I am Julian Hardy, an American journalist.

IZZET.
Ah! from America?

HARDY.
Yes. Shall I tell you something about my country?

FATINITZA.

MY NATIVE LAND.

IZZET.

Very fine sentiments, and I sympathize with them. And so you are an Effendi—who—

HARDY.

Who knows, sees, hears, and listens to everything; puts it on paper; ventilates every question.

IZZET.

A paper ventilator! Aha!

HARDY.

You've said it, Pasha!

IZZET.

Well, and are you going to ventilate me?

HARDY.

The article is ready in my head,—" Izzet Pasha, or the Practical Reform Turk."

IZZET.

Very good! Here's to you, *Hardy Effendi!*

HARDY.

The same to you, old boy. You're a trump of a Pasha! You are making a heaven of earth! What splendid champagne! What an enchanting existence! And this *Kismét*, this delightful *Kismét!*

IZZET.

Yes, Kismét,—neck or nothing.

DUET.—"KISMET."

IZZET.

Every author is, at beginning,
Hopeful ever, hopeless never!

HARDY.

Every maiden, is at beginning,
Timid ever, brazen never!

IZZET.

If then the world the author hisses,
That is his Kismét!

HARDY.

If then the maid risks all in kisses,
That is her Kismét!

IZZET.

If then with trials his life doth fill,

HARDY.

And she for kisses seeking still,

IZZET.

He'll say——

HARDY.

She'll say——

BOTH.

Kismét! Kismét!

IZZET.

Every bride is at first beginning,
Loving ever, saucy never!

HARDY.
Every husband is at beginning,
Happy ever, ugly never!

IZZET.
But when the upper hand she's taking,
That is her Kismét!

HARDY.
He sometimes feels his head is aching.
That is his Kismét!

IZZET.
And yet, while showing her teeth at will,

HARDY.
And he, while rubbing his poor head still,

IZZET.
She'll say——

HARDY.
He'll say——

BOTH.
Kismét! Kismét!

BOTH (*together*).
Modes and women, both are fate—
Ever changeful alike are they;
Drain the cup of joy to-day;
Don't delay, love away!
Who knows what may be soon his Kismét?
Kismét!

HARDY.
Oh, what a pity, Pasha, that the Koran forbids you to show me your harem!

IZZET.
The Koran forbids nothing of the sort!

HARDY.
What! Really?

IZZET.
Haha! No, of course not! [*Merrier.*] We Moslems made the rule ourselves.

HARDY.
Well, if that is so, brother Pasha, then — you know — just give me an introduction to your wives.

IZZET.
Yok! yok! That wouldn't do.

HARDY.
Only think what a chance it is to make you famous! When I sling off an article, "Izzet Pasha's Harem, the Practical Reform Turk " —

IZZET.
Haha! That wouldn't be bad.

HARDY.
I will call you the finest *connoisseur* of feminine beauty.

IZZET.
That's just what I am — you bet!

HARDY.
I will describe the charms of each wife in the most enthusiastic and poetical style.

IZZET.
That *would* be tame. It will be a good advertisement, — give me a chance to sell the whole four of them. The women are about as good as new. So you shall see them, brother.

HARDY.
That's right! Trot 'em out, old boy!

IZZET.
But simply *look* at them. Remember now, simply *look* at them!

HARDY.
I understand. In our exhibitions it always says, "Please do not handle the goods."

IZZET.
Yes, that's what I meant! [*Claps his hands three times.*]

MUSTAPHA (*enters*).
Effendi!

IZZET.
The women!

[MUSTAPHA *takes a set of four bells, each of a different tone, which he sounds during the following.*]

IZZET (*to* HARDY).
Now you shall see how a wise wife knows the tone of her own bell.

HARDY.
By Jove! they are trained like dogs in a circus!

BELL SEXTETTE

NURSIDAH (*enters*).
Bells so silvery, thy sweet ringing
On us calls to be near at hand;
And each fair one is springing
To obey our Pasha's new command.

HARDY.
Thus veiled, they all are alike now to me.

IZZET.
This is Nursidah,—a trifle dear;
Six thousand crowns paid I for her.
ZULEIKA. Bells so silvery, &c.
HARDY. If I mistake not, the lady is fair.

IZZET.
This is Zuleika, both fair and ripe,
For her I did exchange a Turkish pipe.

NURSIDAH & ZULEIKA.
How kind he seems! how gallant and gay!
The stranger hath a right pleasant way.

HARDY. Of envy, worthy you well may be.
IZZET. Just wait a bit—there's more to see.
HARDY. I seem to wander and gaze in a dream.

IZZET
This is Diona, to me of worth;
She came to honor my day of birth.

BESIKA (*enters*).
Silver bell voice, &c. (*As before.*)

HARDY. A piquant set,
In faith, is this quartette!
IZZET. Besika had I in change, well suited,
For one that left here, and thus scooted!

HARDY.
I envy you, as I said before,
How, with so much, can you ask for more?

THE FOUR WIVES.
How kind he seems, &c. (*As before.*)

FATINITZA.

IZZET.

With open mouth he stands—
He looks with surprise at this,
Rolling his eyes in ecstasies:
Therefore, it can't be gainsaid,
Without compare, the choice is made.
    Allah! Allah!
All these fair beauties my treasures are!

HARDY.

How charming a view is this,
That fills the eyes with ecstasies!
With exquisite forms, I find—
Graceful beyond compare, and kind.
    Allah! Allah!
I'd like, most certain, to be a Pasha!

THE FOUR WIVES.

Ah! see how surprised he is!
With his eyes fixed in ecstasies!
All, gallantly, doth he find,
Amiable, charming, fair and kind!
    Allah! Allah!
Leave us not, stranger, now for the war.

IZZET.

He the press makes his profession,
Everything knowing, sees all that's going;
Of views as artist gives expression:
Wisdom e'er showing, judgment bestowing.
I would have him see you all:
Rise and let your veils down fall.

HARDY (*dazzled*).
Ha! How charming a view, &c. (*As before.*)

THE FOUR WIVES & SLAVES.
Ah! see how surprised he is, &c. (*As before.*)

IZZET.

Ah! what says he?
Like a statue he stands! Ha!
How seems it? Have you gazed yet enough?
Of rarest types they are all, indeed!

(*To the wives.*)

Dost love me alone?
Come, speak out, is it true?

WIVES (*shaking their heads negatively*).
Yes! Yes!

IZZET.
They affirm it!

HARDY.
Would kisses from others
Give pleasure to you?

WIVES (*nodding affirmatively*).
No! No!

IZZET.
They deny it.

HARDY.
Virtue is active?

WIVES (*negatively shaking heads*).
Yes! Yes!

HARDY.
And men attractive?

WIVES (*nodding*).
No! No!

HARDY.
You like flirtation?

WIVES (*shaking their heads*).
Yes! Yes!

HARDY.
Mystification?

WIVES (*nodding*).
No! No!

HARDY.

In this case, they're not amiss—
We refuse, but the *no* still means *yes!*
If the other way we go,
We assent, but the *yes* still means *no!*
Many times, as you'll guess,
No is close beside the *yes!*

IZZET.

Ah, women's the same still, wherever you go,
She winks to you *yes*, while she says to you *no!*
The difference between them, amounts but to this:
They say to you *no*, but intend it for *yes!*
    No variation lies
    In nationalities;
From Caucasus to Chili, they're the same!

CHORUS.

Say a *yes* for a *no*, a *no* for a *yes*—
This is the common way with us!

MUSTAPHA.
The festival your highness ordered is ready.

IZZET.
Then bring fair Lydia to me;
The festival's sunshine must she be.

HARDY (*aside*).
'Tis almost time for our friends to come.

(MUSTAPHA *opens the doors.* LYDIA *enters, attended by slaves.*)

IZZET.
Now for the Karagois.

HARDY.
What is that? if I may ask.

IZZET.
Karagois is a shadow play—the comedy of the Moslem.

HARDY.
Aha! By Jove! I breathe freer! What luck!
What splendid material for descriptive writing!

FATINITZA.

LYDIA *(undertone to* HARDY).
Let us pray that the plan of our friends may succeed.
                    HARDY *(the same).*
It is almost time for them. Has Vladimir told you all, princess?
   LYDIA. He has. But now we must be silent.
   IZZET *(aloud).*   Where is Massaldshi?
   MASSALDSHI *(reader of the story to the play).*
Here, exalted sir!
   IZZET. Begin!

(The stage is darkened in front. The curtains in background are opened, revealing a white sheet stretched so as to show the shadows from behind.)

             MASSALDSHI *(reciting).*

"Ben-Jemin and Suréma" is the title of the play
With which I'll entertain you, if so you wish, to-day.
Disturb not my recital by noise or questions tame,
And if you've aught to speak of—well keep still all the same.
Suréma, lovely daughter of Jussuf, the Kabyle,
A child whose sixteen summers did many charms reveal—
Fell deep in love! The object to whom her heart she gave,
Was Ben-Jemin, the handsome, who was, in fact, her slave.
But he had no suspicion where she her love had placed,
Ne'er dreamed that he, her servant, was as her idol graced.
He was so cold, that anger awoke within her heart;
What dame would not be wrathful at such neglectful part?
She shrewdly thus addressed him, "How crimson is your cheek!
You seem unwell and troubled; if ill, what ails you? speak!
I judge that you are feverish, from your unsteady gait;
Sit down near me and rest you, and all your griefs relate."
A Hebrew was Ben-Jemin, Ben-Jochem's son, they say;
Alarmed,—of spies suspicious,—he turned and ran away.
Surprised, enraged, Suréma to angry words gave vent;
Such contumelious action she must and would resent.
She cried, "You bashful Jew boy, hold up, stop, be a man!"
The loved one kept on running, and after him she ran.
Two aged, pious ladies o'erheard what had occurred,
And rushed to tell the father, with many a damning word,
What they themselves had witnessed from their retreat near by.
The prince, at first, believed not that his daughter was so sly,
But when they had convinced him, enraged by what he heard,
He smote all things about him, and tore his hair and beard.
Of his wild beasts, the keeper, a darkey called he there,
With many an angry gesture, and many a vengeful air;
He whisper'd something fearful in his astonish'd ear,
And then his heart grew calmer, his voice more soft and clear.
Suréma found it irksome, and could not long endure
To be angry with her loved one for what he could not cure;
The fire within her bosom could not be quenched at will,
So she made to Ben confession that she adored him still.
But scarcely had the lovers begun to taste their bliss,
And lose their wits and senses in many a loving kiss,
When with roarings loud, terrific, that through the still air rung,
Two wild beasts from the thicket rushed out, and towards them sprung.

*(*BEN-JEMIN *and* SUREMA *flee with genuine screams of terror.* KANTCHUKOFF *and* STEIPANN *appear as shadows with swinging sabres.)*

   IZZET. Two Russians! the play is new and good.
      Make those wild beasts appear—
      That would not be so bad!
   LYDIA *(aside).* At last!
   IZZET. Go on there; don't you interrupt!
   LYDIA *(softly).* On us it smiles again, sweet liberty!
   IZZET. The play is good; ah, ha!
      'Tis good, and makes me laugh!
   RUSSIANS *(outside).* Hurrah! Hurrah!
   LYDIA. Come onward! By your bold deeds
      The victory is completed.
   IZZET. What's that noise—that disturbance?
   LYDIA. Now forward! O soldiers brave!
      My heart exults within me!
   RUSSIANS. Hurrah! Hurrah!
   CHORUS. Hurrah! Hurrah!
   IZZET & TURKS. Allah! Allah!
   VLADIMIR *(enters dressed as an officer).* Lydia, Julian, relief now is here!
             RUSSIANS *(ensemble).*
      Russia, now, in all her splendor shines!
   TURKS. Allah! on these Russian traitors fall!
   GENERAL KANTCHUKOFF. Surrender! resistance is in vain. Let nobody stir from the spot.
   IZZET. This is my Kismét.
   VLADIMIR *(hiding behind* HARDY). For heaven's sake, don't let him recognize me!
   GENERAL. Where is she? Where is Fatinitza?
   HARDY. Fatinitza has been carried off.
   GENERAL. Fatinitza carried off? Just wait, Pasha! for that I annex all your wives!
   ZULEIKA. Exalted sir, we shall follow you with pleasure. *(To* IZZET.) That shall be your punishment, you reform Turk!
   THE OTHER WOMEN. Evett! Evett! Yes! Yes!
   IZZET. Mustapha, persuade them!

MUSTAPHA.
To hear is to obey! [*About to use his whip.*]

GENERAL KANTCHUKOFF (*striking* MUSTAPHA *with the knout*).
Chorrt rasmi! You son of a Turk! [*To the officers*] Take the women with you. And you, Pasha, the knout for you!

IZZET.
Oh, Kismét! Kismét!

ENSEMBLE.

LYDIA & FOUR WIVES.
Oh, how through the golden haze,
Of joy, now stream the brilliant rays!
'Mid clashing of arms around.
Anthems from grateful hearts resound.
Ardor! valor! laurels and bays
Will crown these days.

IZZET.
Oh! Oh!
That infernal Kismét!
Oh! Allah! Oh!

KANTCHUKOFF, HARDY & STEIPANN.
Ah, yes! the whiplash!
So well to the back 'tis adjusted!
All form now in line—
Every corporal,
Captains and majors all
Every general,
And the great Kantchukoff.

[CURTAIN.]

THIRD ACT.

CHIMES OF PEACE.

Odessa. In the summer-palace of Gen. Kantschukoff.

(*When the curtain rises,* LYDIA *with the four women hasten across the scene on balcony. All gaze fixedly off* R., *and wave their handkerchiefs.* LYDIA *comes forward, while the four women remain in the background.*)

BELL ARIA.

LYDIA.

Holy bell! whose peal outringing
Joy is bringing, I feel it flinging
O'er us its spell!
Send thy peace throughout the nation,
The consolation
Of weary hearts.
Chime on gaily; for thy ringing
Hope renewed imparts;
But amid the joy can I rejoice?
Comes to me sweet peace with soothing voice?
Feels my soul in sorrow;
Calm will be the morrow;
Hope and faith smile again.
To this heart will fate my love restore?
When shall I again his face behold?

Will his smile illume this life once more,
Dry my tears that fall untold?
Will those tones to heaven ascending
Bear a word of love for me?

[LYDIA *seats herself. The four women come forward.*]

STEIPANN (*limps in with a cane*).
A guest!

ALL (*joyfully*).
Vladimir! Vladimir!

STEIPANN.
No: his friend, the newspaper-man!

LYDIA.
What fortune! Perhaps he brings glad news.

HARDY (*enters*).
At first glad news, I live; then gladder news, he lives; then the gladdest news of all, he is close by!

FOUR WOMEN.
Allah kerim! he lives!

STEIPANN.
He lives!

LYDIA.
At last, certainty: he lives!

HARDY.
I hastened to come on before, princess, that I might find out the truth about a certain rumor,—that you are betrothed to a Prince Terchi — Shwerchi— (*Sneezes*) Hachoo!

LYDIA.
Swertikoff!

HARDY.
Swertikoff — correct. Is that true?

LYDIA.
Yes and no! My uncle, who has won over the Grand Duchess Imanovna, wants me to marry him!

HARDY.
Poor Vladimir!

LYDIA.
Rather say, "Poor Swertikoff;" for I will never marry him, never!

HARDY.
Good enough! Well, Vladimir has deserved you. With the name Lydia on his lips he wrought heroic deeds at Plevna. You know I was with the Russians all through the siege.

STEIPANN (*grumbling to himself*).
Chorrtu! A reporter there, while I — (*pointing to his maimed foot*).

HARDY.
Well, Steipann, how goes it?

STEIPANN.
Miserably, miserably! as you see. The devilish Turkish bullet! But the fair princess has taken good care of me here in the general's palace.

HARDY.
Well, how is the old gentleman? I hope the course of events has made him forget the divine Fatinitza?

LYDIA.
On the contrary he is possessed with the idea of finding his love again; and only in order to find an excuse to talk constantly about Fatinitza did he allow me to take these poor women into the palace.

FATINITZA.

HARDY.
What! The lovely collection from Izzet Pasha's harem in a Russian edition? *(To LYDIA)* So the old gentleman is determined to marry you off this very day. I see it is high time that we should take an active part.

LYDIA.
But how?

HARDY.
I hardly know how myself as yet. *[Calls]* Steipann!

STEIPANN.
Sir?

HARDY.
Announce me to the general.

STEIPANN.
The general is announcing himself. He has been so ever since the days of Rustchuk. Come, girls, let us get out of his way!

GENERAL KANTCHUKOFF *(enters)*.
Chorrt casnii!! Ten thousand lashes with the knout for this scamp of a chamberlain! What did I say? — ten thousand? No, twenty thousand — a hundred thousand — with the *knout!*

HARDY.
Ah, I see that our friend the general is as strong at his decimals as he was when before Rustchuk.

GENERAL *(enraged).*
Rustchuk! *[Sees HARDY; calms down.]* What! Hardy? *[Warmly]* Ah, my dear friend! welcome to Odessa!

HARDY.
Thank you, general!

GENERAL.
What happy accident brings you hither to-day?

HARDY.
I came on with a part of the Plevna corps to describe their reception home. Six columns by cable!

GENERAL.
Good! Now you can be a witness; but, first, a word to my niece. Lydia Imanovna!

LYDIA.
Uncle?

GENERAL.
Your betrothed, the Prince Swertikoff, has assembled himself in the reception-saloon. It is my wish that you welcome him.

LYDIA.
But, uncle!

GENERAL.
Don't contradict; you know me! Your betrothal is an act of gratitude on my part. Forty years ago he saved my life, when I was a lieutenant in the Caucasus.

HARDY.
If my computations are correct, then the youthful bridegroom must be at least fifty-eight years old.

GENERAL *(with satisfaction).*
You undervalue him. He is sixty-four. A brave man! In saving me, he lost an eye; and a fragment of a shell took away the greater part of his left ear, and made him nearly deaf.

HARDY.
If he is a shelled ear, he must be a cob.

LYDIA.
And you will marry me to such an ancient ruin?

GENERAL.
He is one of the best fellows in all Russia. In the good old days of serfdom he owned sixty thousand souls.

HARDY.
And not much of a body.

LYDIA.
I feel no calling to act the part of ivy to this ruin.

GENERAL.
Sorry for you; but you must marry him.

LYDIA.
I shall scratch out both his eyes

GENERAL.
Impossible! he has only one eye.

LYDIA.
Uncle, you are a monster!

GENERAL.
Many have told me that; but somehow I could never believe it.

LYDIA.
I shall carry my case to the Czar.

GENERAL.
You can do that after the wedding, Lydia Imanovna. I have given my word to Swertikoff. You know me: so go and welcome him.

LYDIA.
Never!

HARDY *(in undertone).*
Obey him, princess; and in the mean while I will try to bring the old gentleman around.

GENERAL.
Do not work me up, Lydia, — and go! Welcome Swertikoff, *[calls after]* and don't forget, — he can only hear with his right ear!

LYDIA.
Well, I will scream such an energetic "no" into it, that that also shall be made deaf. *[Exit.]*

HARDY *(aside).*
Fatinitza must help us again. *[Aloud]* May I know, general, your reason for marrying off the princess so summarily?

GENERAL.
You know it already, sir.

HARDY.
I?

GENERAL.
Fatinitza is the reason.

HARDY *(astonished).*
Oh!

GENERAL.
Yes, my friend, you know that Fatinitza disappeared on that day, and left no trace behind her.

HARDY.
I remember. *[Aside.]* Because she was transformed back to Vladimir.

GENERAL.
Hassan Bey, that Turkish rascal, abducted our.

HARDY.
So they say.

GENERAL.
I know where she went to.

HARDY.
I am curious to hear.

GENERAL.
I have offered a reward of one hundred thousand silver rubles for her. These posters are to be seen on every street-corner throughout the Orient. All at once I received the tidings, "She lives."

HARDY
Really!

GENERAL.
And more: just imagine my insane joy!—she is to be mine this very day.

HARDY.
Who?

GENERAL.
Why, Fatinitza

HARDY (aside).
Can it be that Vladimir is up to another of his mad pranks?

GENERAL.
Vuika, the Bulgarian spy,—the brave fellow!—has discovered her. He has already written me several letters.—this, this, and this here; and ten minutes ago I received these lines. [*Throws all the letters but one on to a table, trembling with excitement.*] Just imagine my unspeakable joy! He writes—he writes: [*attempts to read the letter*] Your Excellence — Your Excellence — Your — [*Takes off his specs.*] I cannot read: the letters dance before my eyes for very joy! [*Gives* HARDY *the letter.*]

HARDY.
Allow me, general. Vuika writes,—

LETTER DUETTINO.

(KANTCHUKOFF *accompanies* HARDY'S *song with animated gestures.*)

HARDY (*reading*).
'Tis now three months that I have wandered,
  Fair Fatinitza's flight to trace—
In Cairo, Smyrna, gold I've squandered,
  And touched at many another place.
And such a dog's life, lone and dreary,
  While seeking her, did I endure;
From land to land I travelled weary,
  At last I found her, fast and sure.

GENERAL.
Oh, Fatinitza!
What handling rough thou didst endure!

HARDY.
And when Isaktscha was subjected,
  The Harem, whence she disappeared;
They sent her to Stamboul, dejected,
  And sold her to a Cadi feared.

GENERAL.
Was sold to a Cadi whose eyes were bleared!

HARDY.
The Cadi failed, and off he scrambles—
  The court condemned him in a flash!
They led her to the market shambles,
  And left her there on sale, for cash!

GENERAL.
Oh, Fatinitza!
How much grief didst thou endure!

HARDY.
The old Bashaw of Negroponto,
  Upon her threw his eyes one day;
He bought—not on his own account though—
  And shipped her off to Tunis' Bey!
The Bey, not long in glad possession,
  Of indigestion died, they say;
The son, who followed in succession,
  To his Mushir gave her away!

GENERAL.
Oh, Fatinitza! how much, &c.

HARDY.
At raffle this Mushir did set her,
  And Aghi-Aga drew the lot;
Next day i.r naught, or scarcely better,
  He swapped her to a Sheik for shot!

GENERAL.
Put up in a raffle's too hard a lot!

HARDY.
'Twas with this last one that I found her,
  And quickly brought her here again;
'Tis strange, with such temptations 'round her,
  She pure and faithful doth remain!

GENERAL.
Oh, Fatinitza!
My love redoubles in my breast!

HARDY.
His love redoubles in his breast!

BOTH.
Oh, Fatinitza! &c.

HARDY (*aside*).
I hardly know what to say to this. [*Aloud*] According to this description Fatinitza appears to have been in pretty brisk demand.

GENERAL.
But, in spite of all, she kept her troth, and withstood the blandishments of all Pashas, Mushirs, and Muftis. And the steamer from Constantinople is due to-day.

HARDY (*aside*).
I shall await the next development with curiosity.

GENERAL.
And so I marry Lydia to the Prince Swertikoff to get her out of my way.

HARDY (*aside*).
Aha!

GENERAL.
You see, two women in the house,—that wouldn't work! But congratulate me.

HARDY.
Certainly, general. I tender you my most heartfelt sympathy,—only—

GENERAL.
Only? *Chorrt rasmi!* What reason is there for an only?

HARDY.
You have perhaps forgotten that Fatinitza has a brother

GRAND TRIO BY FATINITZA, LYDIA, AND JULIAN.
(PATENT APPLIED FOR.)

GENERAL.
Had a brother, — I know, — an officer who fell at Plevna.

HARDY.
Oh, no! he lives, and made a hero of himself at Shipka. He came with the troops to-day.

GENERAL.
Well, so much the better. He shall come to the wedding, and witness our happiness. He belongs to the family.

HARDY (*aside*).
Every thing is all right now! [*Aloud*] May I summon him, general?

GENERAL.
Yes, as soon as possible. As for me, I will ascend to the palace-roof. The fresh air will cool the raging cataract of my excited blood. O Fatinitza! &c.

HARDY (*hurries to balcony, and beckons below*).
There! first he — and now —

[LYDIA *enters and advances.*]

HARDY.
Ah, princess, you are already here! And he will come in a moment!

LYDIA (*joyously*).
Vladimir?

HARDY.
If you follow my directions, he shall be yours this very day.

LYDIA.
Impossible! My uncle has the Grand Duchess Imanovna on his side.

HARDY.
And in my modest self you have the Grand Duke of the Press on your side. Depend upon me!

TRIO.

VLADIMIR.
To this loving heart
I fold thee once more.
O love! again thy form I see:
Naught else is so dear.
Fate no longer I fear,
Since it doth thee restore:
E'en heaven no sweeter bliss can show,
No greater joy bestow!

LYDIA.
I fold thee once more, &c.

HARDY.
Now heart and love and smile:
We'll let them rest a while,
And some attention pay the uncle,
Who's not far away.
Comes he to take his share,
It would my plans betray.

VLADIMIR.
Should all the infernal hosts combine
To part us, her I'd not resign!

LYDIA.
Ere I could see thee turn from me,
Dear love, I fain would die with thee!

HARDY.
She fain would die?
Then die, and end it.
Haha, haha!
First let's agree together
That this is right warm weather.
So, if you think of living,
Some heed to it be giving;
Since these spasms do not increase,
But at the altar's foot will cease.

LYDIA.
Two short moments kindly spare me —
Not too great a boon is this. —
In brief you then shall hear me
Tell him all my heart is his!

HARDY.
Two short minutes, — all straight!
With my watch in hand I'll wait.

LYDIA.
'Tis well! agreed! Two minutes, and no more, I need!
When in the sky the bright stars gleamed,
I thought of thee, and sleeping dreamed;
And as I lay I seemed to hear thy breathing clear,
When horrors dire of battle-strife
I saw appear;
And then the dream to fade did seem,
And I my beating heart could bear!
Tictac, tictac, tic! thus on it went, —
Tictac, tictac, tic, with firm intent!
Ever readily, ever steadily,
Till my breast was bruised and rent.

ALL THREE.
Tictac, tictac, &c.

HARDY.
See, the time's already wasted;
Let us now some wisdom show.
Thou art otherwise invested;
She another's bride must go!

VLADIMIR.
Alas! speak: is this truely so?

LYDIA.
Ah! 'tis my uncles's will, you know.

HARDY.
Yes, yes, the case is very strange!
Forgetful your wits are,
That you are Fatinitza.
This uncle will you marry.

VLADIMIR.
Then I'm to be the bride!

HARDY.
Of course, you are the bride!

LYDIA.
His bride?

HARDY.
Why, yes; he will you wed.
Thou'lt be his bride! Ha, ha!

VLADIMIR.
I wed?

ALL THREE.
Hahaha! ha, ha, ha!

VLADIMIR.
Two minutes more then wilt thou spare me?
Not too much to ask is this;
In brief, you then shall hear me
Tell her what my heart's state is.

HARDY.
Well, so be it: all right!
But be punctual to your word!

VLADIMIR.
I swear to you by cross and sword,
Though distance did us part,
I was with thee mind and heart
'Mid the flash of the swords, meeting in bold hostile encounter
When the flash of the trumpet-call sounded all else above.
Hurrah! in the heart of the fray,
Girdled by blood, rapine, and slaughter,
I beheld, shining clear and bright,
The fair star of our love

And whether waves of battle-tide
Came by turns advancing on,
Or backward flowed on every side,
Still my thoughts were full of thee.
A voice in whisper said to me,
   March forward fearlessly!
   Now thy valor prove:
   That standard-bearer free
   Leading thee is love!
   Forward, with sword in hand!
   Smite the hostile band!
   A heart indeed
   Shall be the conqueror's meed!

ALL.
March, &c.

MARCH FORWARD FEARLESSLY.

March forward fear-less-ly, Now thy val-or prove; That standard-bear-er free Lead-ing thee, is love! For-ward, with sword in hand, Smite the hos-tile band! A heart, in-deed, shall be the conqu'ror's meed!

[LYDIA exit. VLADIMIR accompanies her.]

HARDY.
Now, Vladimir, my boy, arm yourself with all the pride of your manhood. The general is coming. I will prompt you what to say.

GENERAL (enters).
Smoke! smoke!

HARDY.
Where?

GENERAL.
The steamer which brings me my darling. I hasten to meet her. [Going, sees VLADIMIR.] Ha! 'tis she—no, he—she in the masculine,—Fatinitza!

HARDY (*introducing him*).
Lieut. Vladimir Samoiloff!

VLADIMIR (*salutes*).
General!

GENERAL.
General? Oh, get out! none of that to me! Brother-in-law! Come to my arms, my boy! [*Embraces him heartily.* To HARDY] Does he know?

HARDY.
No.

GENERAL.
Then do not swoon with joy, youngster: in a few minutes more you shall see her again.

VLADIMIR.
Whom?

GENERAL.
Why, Fatinitza, — your sister!

VLADIMIR.
I don't believe it! I don't believe it!

HARDY (*in undertone to* VLADIMIR).
You had better believe it!

GENERAL.
You shall know all! Of course you shall be my adjutant with the rank of major.

VLADIMIR.
Major?

GENERAL.
Well, then, if that is not enough, I'll make it colonel.

VLADIMIR (*joyfully*).
Colonel! colonel! O general!

GENERAL.
Say no more! You must be colonel willy nilly! Chorrt vasmi! Discipline must be maintained. And you must live here with us; must never leave us.

VLADIMIR.
Oh, what happiness!

GENERAL.
But at first (*ceremoniously*), colonel, have you parents?

VLADIMIR.
Alas, I am an orphan!

GENERAL.
So you are head of the family!

VLADIMIR.
Yes.

GENERAL.
Then I have the honor to ask you for the hand of your sister, Fatinitza.

HARDY (*undertone*).
Say no; say she is engaged.

VLADIMIR.
She is engaged.

GENERAL.
Oh, I'll fix that! She loves me.

VLADIMIR.
Impossible!

GENERAL.
Barbarian! How can you compel your sister to enter into a repulsive marriage?

HARDY.
But, general, that is the way you serve the princess.

GENERAL.
That is quite another thing: I am her uncle.

VLADIMIR.
And I her brother.

GENERAL.
Oh, don't be obstinate, colonel. Come! you consent. Just help me out of this, Hardy. Fatinitza must be mine at any price. He may demand what he will: I will consent.

HARDY (*in undertone*).
Ask for Lydia now.

VLADIMIR.
Dare I venture?

GENERAL.
Venture all you want.

VLADIMIR.
You will be angry.

GENERAL.
I angry? Do I look like a man who would get angry? [*Wrathful.*] Chorrtu! and when I say at that, that I shall not be angry. Out with it!

VLADIMIR.
Well, then, I love the Princess Lydia Imanovna, and ask for her hand.

GENERAL (*enraged*).
Chorrt rasmi! The brass of the fellow! A miserable lieutenant presumes —

HARDY.
But he is a colonel.

GENERAL.
Not yet. [*Rushes at* VLADIMIR *in rage.*] And for his impertinence he shall —

HARDY.
Look out! you are getting excited.

GENERAL (*calmer*).
Oh, no! You see I am calm, very calm.

VLADIMIR.
Then you say yes.

GENERAL.
No! the marriage is impossible. My niece is betrothed.

VLADIMIR.
So is Fatinitza.

GENERAL.
I am bound by my word.

VLADIMIR.
I too.

HARDY.
Then how would it be if both gentlemen should try to induce the respective bridegrooms to withdraw?

GENERAL.
Very well! Then kick your man out of doors.

VLADIMIR.
You do the same with yours.

GENERAL.
Yes; that is, no. I will find another way. My friend Swertikoff cannot demand that Lydia should sacrifice herself to a deaf old jackass like him.

VLADIMIR.
And Capt. Vasil is a too sensible man not to see that if Fatinitza loves you —

GENERAL.
Yes, she does love me. And if you will swear —

VLADIMIR.
What, general?

GENERAL.
That I shall have your sister —

VLADIMIR.
If you can find her — yes!

GENERAL (aside).
I have her at hand.

HARDY.
And if Fatinitza loves you —

GENERAL.
She loves me madly.

VLADIMIR.
And if she will say that in my presence —

GENERAL.
She will! she will!

VLADIMIR.
Then I will break off her engagement.

GENERAL.
And I that of my niece — at once! [Runs to door, and calls] Lydia!

[LYDIA enters in bridal dress, attended by the four women.]

GENERAL.
Come nearer, my child. What I have once determined stands fast, — fast as iron. No contradiction! you shall not marry the Prince Swertikoff!

LYDIA.
Why not, uncle?

GENERAL.
The fool is too old for you. You will please make up your mind at once to marry Colonel Vladimir Samoiloff, who, I have reason to believe, is somewhat younger.

HARDY (undertone to LYDIA).
Refuse.

LYDIA.
Marry him? Why?

GENERAL.
No why nor wherefore. You will please to love him at once, and make him happy. Embrace your betrothed! (In undertone to HARDY) They must be married before Fatinitza arrives!

STEIPANN (enters R.).
The priest and the guests!

[Priest and guests enter.]

GENERAL.
Welcome! Here is the bride! here is the bridegroom! Here you have my blessing; and now — right-about face — march! — into the chapel with you! When you are married, then I will introduce my bride to you. (Aside) No doubt of it: these tones announce the arrival of the fair Fatinitza! [Goes to background excitedly. The wedding procession forms.]

HARDY (to VLADIMIR).
Make use of the favorable opportunity. I will ward off the recoil! Have you still the engagement-ring which the general placed on Fatinitza's finger?

VLADIMIR.
Here it is. [Gives it to him.]

HARDY.
Good enough! I will take care of the rest. [Exit hurriedly.]

GENERAL (who stands on the balcony, and beckons down below, calls back).
What! are you not coupled yet? Forwards. double-quick — march!

[The wedding procession marches into the chapel.]

FINALE.

(GENERAL K., VUIKA, Georgians, Russians, male and female servants. Afterwards HARDY. At last VLADIMIR, LYDIA, and guests. VUIKA enters with chorus; behind him four negro boys bearing a palanquin, which they hold above the false FATINITZA, who is splendidly arrayed and closely veiled.

CHORUS.

Praise and honors high!
To foreign charms we sing;
  Orders thus our chief commander!
From far distant shores, a Russ,
  She has come to us.
Praises sing, and sweet flowers bring;
  Orders thus our chief commander
In her face shines every grace,
  Says the chief commander,
Virgin pure, of noble race,
  Says the chief commander;
Bride, fresh and fair as she,
  Or maiden, there cannot be—no!
Brightly her sweet smile beamed,
  A warrior's heart subduing;
Won by her modest mien,
  Her smile was his undoing!
    Fatinitza! Fatinitza!
To thy charms we praises sing;
Honors and garlands of flowers to thee we bring,
    Thus orders our commander!

GENERAL (approaches the stranger).
At last I shall behold thy lovely face again. Unveil her. Chorri vasmi! A negress! Is it possible that you have grown black in the face all for love of me? Fatinitza! is it you?

VUIKA.
Her name is Fatinitza, sir: it is she.

HARDY (enters).
No! it is not she! You are a pack of miserable swindlers; for here — here is a letter from the genuine Fatinitza.

GENERAL.
A letter? Quick! quick! [Breaks the seal hastily — reads] "Beloved, when you receive these lines I shall no longer be among the living. My ardent longing for you has brought me to an early grave. I commit my dear brother Vladimir to your keeping. I enclose my engagement-ring, and regard

myself as your betrothed on the other side. My last breath shall be the sweet name, Timofey Kantchukoff. Yours truly, Fatinitza."

GENERAL (*repeats the refrain*).
Fatinitza! Fatinitza! &c.
By thunder! I am deeply moved. What woman e'er so truly loved as to die with longing for one she missed?

HARDY.
But one [*to audience*] *that never did exist!* [*At this moment* STEIPANN *enters with the four women and the wedding guests; then* VLADIMIR *and* LYDIA.] The wedding is over! Here is the happy pair!

VLADIMIR (*to* HARDY).
What have you done with Fatinitza?

HARDY (*to* VLADIMIR.)
Killed her off. She'll never bother us again.

VLADIMIR (*to* HARDY).
Thank heaven! we're rid of her at last.

GENERAL.
Come to my heart! Be happy!

CLOSING SONG.

LYDIA & VLADIMIR.
Love's holy vow unites us now!
March forward, fearlessly, &c.
HARDY. Ta, ta, ra, ta, ra, &c.
CHORUS. A faithful heart, a prize indeed!
Is surely now the victor's meed.

[END.]

"KISMET" DUET BY THE PASHA AND THE REPORTER.
(PATENT APPLIED FOR.)

INTRODUCTION OF THE REPORTER TO THE PASHA'S WIVES.
(PATENT APPLIED FOR.)

www.ingramcontent.com/pod-product-compliance
Lightning Source LLC
Chambersburg PA
CBHW030709110426
42739CB00031B/1445